ROGUE: THE WEALTH GENERATION BLUEPRINT

A FRAMEWORK FOR ACHIEVING FINANCIAL FREEDOM AND BUILD WEALTH FOR LIFE

STEFAN KUEGLER

For more information, email skuegler@gmail.com.

ISBN: 979-8-90057-399-1 - Ebook
ISBN: 979-8-90057-400-4 - Paperback

To Tania for always believing in me and my thoughts

GET YOUR FREE GIFT!

To get the best experience with this book, I've found readers who download and use templates and resources I've created to help them can implement faster and take the next steps needed to be becoming wealthy.

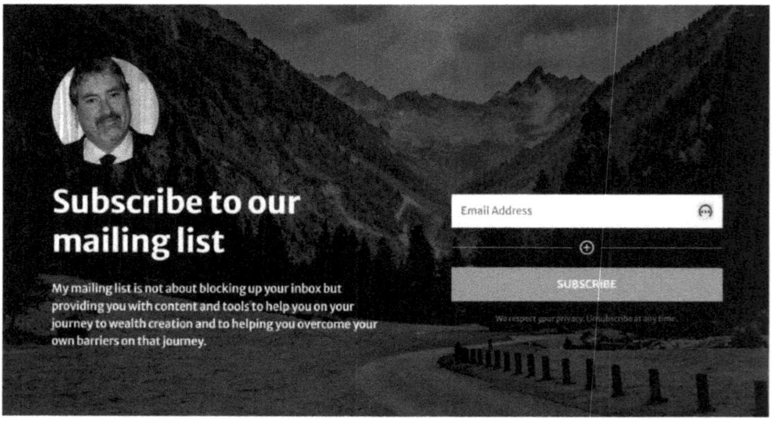

You can join on the page below and I will send you both templates and a monthly newsletter:

https://stefan-kuegler.kit.com/c43ad7ed09

CONTENTS

INTRODUCTION

Though you cannot go back and make a brand-new start, my friend, you can start now, and make a brand-new end.

—Anonymous

My Why

Not to disappoint people too much, but this is not a book about *Star Wars* and *Rogue One.*

It's yet another book about goals and being a success. So why is this one different?

At the start of this process, I asked myself that. A lot of books written about wealth creation are from Fortune 500 executives that have made an enormous amount of wealth. I'm not one of those people, so my advice (hopefully) is a bit more approachable for the average person. I have accumulated a lot of knowledge in my twenty-five years in the finance sector. Today, I am financially free, and I don't have to work anymore. My goal was to be financially free at fifty—which I achieved.I've invested many thousands of hours in learning about financial freedom through books, conferences, seminars, and courses.

I've also spoken to people about their financial success (or lack thereof), and I noticed there were a few elements that we always came back to when I was helping them. These were not difficult elements but were items that were not taught at school and were potentially not passed on through parents. I found that there was a gap in the educational system in teaching people about financial literacy and wealth creation. I had done this informally for a while, but now I wanted to do more in this field.

I work with people to help get them on the road to wealth creation and financial success. I teach them the basics and then allow them to go on their own journeys, making sure that I guide them as much or as little as they need. I offer them a safe harbour to come back to if they need help.

I studied as a statistician with a bachelor's degree in mathematics and then subsequently for a diploma of accounting. I've taken taxation courses, numerous courses on wealth creation, share trading, property development, property management, and property investing. I've completed these in both Australia and the UK. I've talked to a lot of people who are successful in those areas and learned from them. My goal is to communicate this information so it's accessible and easy to understand. I want to provide a framework for other people to follow, to give them some steps to help reach their financial freedom like I did. Mostly, I want to give people choices because that is what money can provide. The choices to do what you want. To be where you want. To have what you want.

Everybody deserves a chance to live their best life, and for most people, that starts with money and security. It builds into bigger things from there. I want to set you on the path to live your dreams and goals.

When I worked at a charity focused on financial literacy, we saw people who had massive amounts of debt. They were struggling with the simplest concepts of financial literacy because nobody had ever taught them. When we opened their eyes to a few little things that were possible once they had a core grasp of financial literacy, it was amazing how much transformation occurred. We set them on a path and then walked alongside them to make sure that they kept to that course.

That's what I'm hoping this book will do as well: Set you on a path and guide you along the way.

I'm writing this book because of the feeling I had when I finally realized that I'd reached this goal. It's a feeling that I want everybody to experience. After my achievement, I had a real sense of pride, achievement, and success.

Before we go any further, I want to discuss what I mean by "wealth." This term can mean different things to different people. Through studying my own experience and the experiences of people I've worked with, I feel there are three levels of wealth.

1. Material wealth: This is the wealth of having things, items, and stuff. This includes what we accumulate and the things we buy ourselves.
2. Financial wealth: This is the money we have access to and the wealth we have stored away for the future
3. Purposeful wealth: This is the wealth aligned with our purpose in life and the satisfaction of helping others.

Each stage is something you go through, and this book is my way of helping others to move along on their journeys.

This book contains lessons and actions to help you along the second and third elements of wealth creation—the financial and purposeful.

There is a reason why, once they have achieved financial wealth, successful businesspeople, gurus, or leadership experts talk about giving back or helping others. This is the third level of wealth creation—being a philanthropist. However, they are only able to do this once they have stable and secure financial situations.

Everybody should have the opportunity to live the life of their dreams, but it starts with financial wealth and builds into the life they want to live.

A First Question

What is the first thing people think when they hear "wealth creation"?

Some hear that term and dive into shares, property, savings, or whatever other investment they think others would be impressed by. Crypto, maybe. What is the next big investment vehicle of the moment?

We want the work to be done for us, so we jump into the next big thing, hoping that it will give us our financial freedom. We are more interested in where we're going to put our money rather than all the other work that needs to go before that. We put the action before education or knowledge. I realize that we all want to get going with building our wealth, but sometimes jumping into the deep end can be detrimental to our long-term goals.

I want to get people to start at the basics so they have realistic chances of reaching their wealth-creation goals. This book is built around the acronym ROGUE (which we will dive more into momentarily). However, the word itself just so happens to have the sentiment that you need. You need to be a bit of a rogue.

There are a couple of things that a rogue is known for. The *Cambridge English Dictionary* defines a rogue[1] as "a person who behaves badly but who you still like" "The lovable rogue" is often quoted or expressed. In this case, we have a similar feeling; the material is something different but still something we want to do or be involved in.

I used to be called a rogue cowboy in one of my jobs, and I quite liked that because it meant I was somebody who thought and acted unconventionally. Like Thomas Edison said: "I have not failed. I've just found ten thousand ways that won't work."

That's what you're doing when you're going through this idea of ROGUE. You must do something differently. You must think slightly differently. You must be different.

With ROGUE, I have put into an acronym the steps required to build wealth. It works for all types of wealth, as I defined it earlier in the introduction, and provides steps to lead you on your path. For this book, we will focus on building financial wealth, but the steps can also be used for any other type of wealth or other ideas.

You also need to be aware of who you are and what your core values are. Your core principles. Your core morals. These are the things that you are, and they generally stay constant. Even if you're young, these values are often set in place when you are a child by watching parents and other adults around you. You'll have developed a lot of your core values from your upbringing and the people around you.

---

1 https://dictionary.cambridge.org/dictionary/english/rogue

What Is ROGUE?

ROGUE stands for:

- **Reason.** You need to have a strong why. You need to have something driving you. You need something that you believe in. You need something that will keep you inspired for your wealth creation journey.
- **Organization.** You need organized action toward your Reason. If you're not aiming at something, you'll hit nothing every time.
- **Gratitude.** You need to be thankful; you need to have that positive attitude. Staying positive is an important part to overcome a lot of hurdles that will be put in your path. So how do we get that? What are some of the ways that we can be grateful for what we have so that we're not constantly looking over the fence at our neighbor's greener grass? Through Gratitude, we also get clarity on what matters to us and what things give us energy.
- **(U) You.** This is about working on yourself and your growth as you move toward fulfilling your reason. There will be a lot of obstacles when striving to reach your Reason. This section is about helping you spot those obstacles so you can reach your goal. We will also investigate your values, thoughts, and feelings around wealth and being wealthy. You need to be congruent in actions, thoughts, and emotions to be wealthy.
- **Endurance.** There is one thing every Reason needs—time. Time to learn. Time to make mistakes. Endurance is making sure you are committed to the long game and sticking to your reason till you get there.

Throughout this book, I'm going to use my "financially free at fifty" goal. It might not sound like something you want to do, or it might sound "small." But that was my wealth-creation goal. I didn't want to work anymore after that point in time, and I'll talk about how I did that and how ROGUE helped me.

I ran a well-being study[2] for a government organization, and through that I realized that although people, up to a point, want to have some money, once they get to a certain point, money becomes irrelevant, and they need bigger reasons. Well-being is not just about the money you have but also what money allows you to do. That's why your "why" can't just be a money target.

There is one rule around wealth creation. If you follow that for all your life, you will have wealth.

Wealth = Income—Expenses

By the way, this needs to be a positive number. If your expenses are greater than your income, then you won't create wealth. If your income is greater than your expenses, then you have the starting point for wealth creation. It's that simple.

I hope through this book that you understand that wealth creation isn't about which shares you pick, but the thoughts that you have around wealth creation.

Each chapter will be detailing a different section of ROGUE. We will go through the idea of each chapter, building out the overview

2 A well-being study is a systematic investigation into the holistic, positive state of individuals or groups, focusing on physical, mental, and social health rather than just the absence of illness. These studies measure subjective life satisfaction, positive emotions, and functioning, often using surveys to assess quality of life.

I described in the introduction and then expanding on these thoughts and giving instructions on how to start on your journey for each section.

Coaching Journey

In each chapter, we will mimic a real coaching session based on my experience as a coach and go through some of the basic responses I have had when working through money issues with people. We will follow the framework of ROGUE to build the wealth journey for Matthew, with his mentor. This provides other examples for each section and gives a more conversational view on creating wealth with support.

Sometimes something new can cause hesitation, fear, and the feeling that "I don't need help." A mentor or coach can help keep you on track and provide good support and knowledge. I've included this coaching journey to show how the interaction between coach and coachee might look.

Sometimes the session might go over a few weeks as Matthew goes off and does some work on the questions set by his mentor, and we then rejoin the thoughts on that topic. Every element of ROGUE requires multiple sessions to really get embedded.

I have used Matthew as the name of the individual engaged in the mentoring journey; however, I encourage you to put yourself in his shoes.

At the end of each chapter, I will provide a starting exercise to help you begin your own journey toward wealth creation.

Enjoy!

CHAPTER 1
REASON

The two most important days in your life are the day you are born and the day you find out why.

—Mark Twain

The first section, (R), stands for Reason; this may also be referred to as goals, vision, or purpose. There are various ways to articulate this idea. Everybody has dreams. Everybody has goals. Everybody has an ideal life in mind. In this first chapter, we will discover why a Reason is important. We will delve into how to create one and how to make it come alive in a way that will inspire you.

My Story

When I was twenty-five, my Reason that I set myself was to be financially free at fifty. The retirement age was set by the government at sixty-five (it is now sixty-seven and creeping upward), but I wanted to live more of my life rather than be chained to a career. I would give myself time to build wealth and then enjoy that wealth while still in some physically strong capacity.

I set this goal coming out of university. Ahead of me, I saw the work and the stress stretching out over the years. I knew I would have to go through some of it, but I didn't want to go through it forever. I also wanted to make sure that I had something to look forward to at the end of those years.

In Australia, we have something called superannuation—putting money away now so in the future, you have money to live on in retirement. This is similar to the 401(k) plan or IRA in the United States or the pension (SIPP) in the UK. When I was younger, most people were on the aged pension, but there was talk that it might not be there in the future. The government might run out of money. Superannuation was supposed to be the fix for citizens so they could retire in comfort. There was a lot of fear and uncertainty.

I didn't want to leave my financial freedom or my retirement years to the unknown. If I had relied on superannuation, I wouldn't really have enough, and I wouldn't be able to live financially free at fifty. (The earliest age you can access superannuation money is sixty.)

I wanted to take my future into my own hands. However, there was one problem, and not a small one either: I didn't have a clue what I was doing. I didn't have an idea or number in mind. I didn't know how much it cost to live. I was a graduate with a new job on the horizon, living at home with my parents. What did I know about the cost of living? I eventually asked myself the question: What did being financially free mean to me?

I tried to imagine what my life might be like at fifty. Why fifty? I didn't think about the age much—it was a nice round number, and it was a long way off in the future. It was also around the time my father "retired" from his formal career.

I didn't have a partner but thought I'd have a family. What else?

I'd need money.

I looked at my parents. What were they doing? And thinking? My parents at this stage had invested a little bit in property. My dad had dabbled in shares. They were good savers and thrifty people. And so that started me on that journey. I saw my parents preparing for when they "retired" but also enjoying their time now by playing golf and enjoying travel. They had no fixed goal but knew it would evolve. They were a guide to me.

In developing a vision for financial independence, I understood it to be a long-term endeavour requiring substantial learning. So why did I choose a Reason like "being financially free at fifty"? I needed something bigger to guide my decisions and thinking over the short and long term. I could be impulsive, but I also knew I wanted more from life than just working for the next forty years (like most people). I saw people who were enjoying retirement and people who were surviving retirement. I didn't want to be one of the latter.

Why Do We Need a Reason?

One of my favourite quotes is from *Alice's Adventures in Wonderland*[3] from the Cheshire Cat.

> Alice came to a fork in the road. "Which road do I take?" she asked.
>
> "Where do you want to go?" responded the Cheshire Cat.
>
> "I don't know," Alice answered.
>
> "Then," said the cat, "it doesn't matter as any road will take you there."

---

3 *Alice' s Adventures in Wonderland*—Lewis Carroll.

Crafting a Reason requires dedicated time and introspection. The first step is to find a quiet space to truly reflect on your life and aspirations. This isn't about setting simple targets like acquiring a certain amount of money—a goal that can feel uninspiring and hollow. Instead, allow yourself the freedom to dream without constraints.

Spend time contemplating what you want your life to look like. Write down anything that comes to mind. Imagine grand goals—whether it's traveling to a hundred countries, climbing the highest mountain on each continent, or becoming an expert in a field you're passionate about. Let your aspirations be as expansive as possible.

In my case, some of my aspirations came from my first trip by myself to Europe. I loved the idea of traveling, meeting people, and just enjoying days in beautiful places. As I grew as a person, I wanted to inspire people as I was inspired by authors and speakers. I trained as a life Coach to help people become their best. I saw wealth in abundance but not an abundant number of people enjoying it, only a select few. I wanted to change that in some way.

The reason this is required is that during the course of your journey, you will hit roadblocks, hurdles, and frustrations, and you need something big to help you keep going. You need to have a Reason to keep getting out of bed. A Reason to keep living within your means. Without your Reason, life has a habit of just pulling you back into mire. You need something to keep your head clear and focused on your purpose.

Questions to Help Identify Your Reason

How do you go about finding your Reason?

This is the most difficult stage, and it is something that you will come back to throughout your journey. As you start to move through your journey to complete your Reason, new thoughts and new experiences will bring you back to your Reason to clarify, enhance, and streamline your thoughts around it.

But first, how do we start?

This is a long process and might require you to take some time out of your busy schedule to sit down and ask yourself a few questions, to explore the answers that come to you. Some answers might be initial thoughts but may be irrelevant until you dig a little deeper; some answers will get to the heart of the issue straightaway.

Be kind to yourself on this part of the journey, and remember that there is no wrong answer and no wrong thought. Do not limit yourself. Let yourself be guided by your emotions as much as your logical thoughts.

Think about these questions:

- If money and time were not important, what would you be doing now?
- If you could study anything, what would it be? Why?
- What tasks, when completed, have given you a deep sense of satisfaction?
- In what activities do you completely lose track of time? Which ones can you do for hours on end without exhaustion or frustration?
- What would you do for free if you could?

- Whom do you like to work with? How do you like to work?
- What places, sights, and scenes would you like to see yourself in?
- If you were given another twenty-four hours each week, what would you spend it on?
- If you were given a million dollars to live on, what would you do with your time?
- If you could volunteer in any location for anything, what would it be?

Answering the questions above is the first step. You might have some vague answers; you might have some very detailed answers. It sometimes depends. Sometimes you need to allow the questions to rattle around in your mind for a few days to come up with something.

Whatever your answers, you need to move onto the next stage.

The Five Whys

The Five Whys[4] is a technique to explore and discover the root cause of a particular problem. The primary technique is to repeat the question "Why?" five times (or more if needed), each time directing the current "why" to the answer of the previous "why."

The method asserts that the answer to the final "why" asked in this manner should reveal the root cause of the problem. Although the Five Whys technique is mostly used in production or manufacturing, it can be used in any setting.

4 The technique was described by Taiichi Ohno at Toyota Motor Corporation. As described here: https://en.wikipedia.org/wiki/Five_whys

An example of a problem is: "I don't like saving."

- Why? *I don't have enough money.*
- Why? *I need money for other things.*
- Why? *The other things make me feel good.*
- Why? *I have little to celebrate in my life, so I need some small parts of joy.*
- Why? *I feel I have underachieved and fear I'm never going to reach my potential.*

This example is very close to how I felt about savings and the process I had to understand as I went through to develop some of my thinking.

How does this help in creating your Reason?

We also want to get to the root cause of our Reason for wanting to do things or understand why the answers given above were so important or at least felt right. We want to understand the underlying dynamics so we can make a more powerful and clearer Reason for ourselves. If we make it vague, then we might not have much skin in the game, and we can lose interest quickly. However, if we have something more succinct and meaningful, then it is difficult to brush it aside, and we will feel more connected to our Reason. Remember, our Reason is our guiding principle and our motivation for getting up in the morning, so it has to speak to us on many levels.

So how to begin? Let's go through another example.

You have your answer (from the questions above) before you—let's say it is "I want to volunteer at my local charity."

Ask yourself the first why.

Why do you want to volunteer at the charity?

Maybe it's because you want to give back to the community.

Then again.

Why do you want to give back to the community?

Maybe it's because other people have helped you in the past, and you were thankful that there were people that cared for you.

And again.

Why was that important to you—that people cared for you?

You keep on going until you ask yourself Five Whys, and at the end, you normally come to the real reason for the initial statement. The reason this is so important is that it goes to the deep levels of our emotions and experience, and we feel a deep connection to it.

In the above example, you might find out that you don't want people to feel alone (like you once did), or that you felt so overwhelmed, you couldn't do anything until someone helped (and you don't want anyone else to experience that), or any other number of reasons. It will be personal, and it will be based on your own experience.

Once you have done the Five Whys with each of your answers, let them sit for a while.

How do those answers feel now? Have you been honest with yourself? Do they resonate on a deep level? Do you feel emotional just thinking about them?

Do you feel congruent when you think about it? And what do we mean by "congruent"?

"Congruence of being"[5] refers to the alignment between a person's actions, thoughts, and feelings. It represents authenticity, where one's inner thoughts and feelings match their outward actions and expressions. This can lead to better self-esteem and self-trust, which can lead to other external factors like better relationships, reduced stress, and more effective communication.

"Incongruence" occurs when there is a significant gap between (mostly) your feelings and your actions, often leading to defensive behavior, anxiety, and a feeling of being "out of sync."

Being congruent means that we have alignment across what we say, how we feel, and what we do. If one of these is out of alignment, then we will start to self-sabotage or find reasons not to do things.

Once you have your Reason and feel in sync with it, we need to bring it to life so that you see and hear it every day, and so that it becomes a part of you. Having your Reason in your head does not put it front and center; you need to have your Reason where it is within easy reach and is accessible. This will form your guide through your life and provide you with your power to resist distraction, keep going upward, and make aligned decisions for your life.

5 Term coined by psychologist Carl Rogers. As described here: https://en.wikipedia.org/wiki/Carl_Rogers#Incongruity

Four Approaches to Bring Your Reason to Life

Everything in our lives happens twice: first in our minds, then in our physical reality.

—Anonymous

Approach 1: Visualization

You can do visualizations of your Reason. Visualize it, visualize it, visualize it. Spend some time immersing yourself in your vision. Talk it through out loud. Understand it. Really make it a part of you.

The more you do it, and the more vivid it becomes, the more real it feels. And when something feels real, you start to act as if it's already happening. That's when the magic happens.

Approach 2: Vision Board

The approach is a vision board. This can be on cardboard, or you can create a digital version. Some people emphasize words; some people emphasize pictures.

Some thoughts on how to construct a vision board—either on paper or digitally:

- Create sections on the area of your vision board based on your Reason.
    - Mark them out into topics such as relationship, finance, hobbies, faith/spiritualism, holidays, etcetera.
- Now ask yourself some questions on each topic to find an appropriate picture and get more detailed information based on your Reason:
    - What do your relationships look like?
    - Do you have a picture of that house you want to live in?
    - What are the things that you're doing that make you happy?
    - What are your investments?
    - What does your bank account balance look like?

    - Are you in a team or by yourself?
    - What is your work?
    - What are the hobbies that you're doing or the other activities that you're involved in?
    - Do you want to volunteer?
    - What other things are important to include?
- Now find some pictures that represent the answers to your questions for each section:
    - Picture of you and your future partner or your current partner.
    - Picture of that house you want to live in.
    - Picture of an organization you want to be a part of.
    - Pictures of sport you are doing or watching.
    - Find a picture of whatever fits into your Reason and put it on the board.

Remember, there is no right or wrong at this stage, this is your why and your dreams.

Approach 3: Mantra or Statement

The third way to pursue your reason is to make a short statement or a mantra. I used this method.

Your mantra can be something very simple: one phrase, one line, or even one word. Something like: "I want to retire at fifty." You might have something more specific: "I want to retire at fifty and live in Jamaica." Or: "I want to own ten properties earning $5,000 per month in rental returns." Or: "I want to be debt-free in two years." If you are starting small first, you can make it whatever you need it to be. And you can develop it as you reach the goals.

When I was going through this process, one of mine was "I want to be financially free at fifty." For me it meant getting away from work, doing my own thing, and being financially independent.

It also means that when you're doing something you can phrase it as a question when you're trying to decide: "Will this [*insert action here*] get me to be able to retire by the time I'm fifty?"

This question will allow you to focus on whether the activity in question will get you closer to your Reason. Depending on the answer, you can then either do or not do the activity.

Approach 4: Spoken Dream

Lastly, consider the "Spoken Reason" approach. Record yourself describing your reason in detail. A few tips for creating the recording:

- Don't go ad-lib for the final recording.
  - You can make some notes ad-lib, but never use this approach for the final version.
- Make notes of the things you want to include—more is definitely better.
- Read it through a few times before you commit it to a recording.
- Make sure you cover all the senses when describing your Reason.
- Use pauses to allow your future listening self to imagine the "picture."

Regularly listening to this recording can reinforce your vision, keeping it fresh and motivating. It also allows for adaptation and refinement as your perspective evolves. You can even pretend like it's your future self talking back to you. It doesn't have to be a day in the life, just sharing what you expect to see, do, and be someday.

This recording should be in an easy to find location so you can listen to it often, preferably at least once a week. Listen, absorb, and feel your words.

By utilizing these methods, you can create a vision that is both inspiring and actionable. This is the first step in taking full responsibility for your life and shaping it according to your deepest desires. Embrace the journey of discovering your reason, and let it guide you toward a fulfilling and purpose-driven life.

Responsibility and Belief

Once you've got your reason, there are two things necessary to embed these into your thinking: responsibility for it and belief in it. That means when something goes wrong, you take 100 percent responsibility and say, "What could I have done better? How could I have managed that situation better? What went wrong, and what's my part?" If we're constantly pushing out to somebody else or blaming somebody else, we're pushing away that responsibility.

This is about *your* Reason. Your goal. You're taking 100 percent ownership of it. This means you are responsible for the decisions, the outcomes, and the mistakes. When something goes wrong, owe it and resolve it. You cannot go into the "blame game." It leads nowhere and can alienate people, and negative thoughts can start. You made that decision. If something goes wrong, the objective is to learn from that decision. Key questions to ask are:

- What happened?

- Why didn't it work out?
- Was I too passive in the decision?
- Did I not make the decision but just let it happen?
- Did I not research the choices enough?
- Was I not using the most up-to-date information?
- Did I not have all the facts?

When it comes to saving or later on to investing, you need to be present. This is not head-in-the-sand time. This is your money.

You left it with somebody else and hoped for the best. That's not ownership, and that's not responsibility. That's just wishful thinking. Was there something else that you could have done? Could you have talked to them a little bit more? Could you have changed the mix of the portfolio? If you knew something was going to happen, maybe you could have moved into property instead of just shares. Always think that you are the one who's taking responsibility for this wealth creation goal.

The second thing you must embed into your thinking is belief. Once you have your reason, you've got to believe that you are going to get there. Our discussion of Endurance (chapter 5) will cover some of this and what will help. However, you need to understand yourself and understand that you will have doubts. This is natural. Maybe you have tried to achieve the goal before. Maybe you didn't get there last time.

A simple truth: Most people try to reach the same goal multiple times. The main reason that it can fail is your belief in yourself or the goal was not strong enough. This can be valuable learning material, and we need to think differently about this "failure." We need to ask questions:

- What did you do in those instances that were going to get you to your goal?
- What didn't you do that you needed to do?
- Did you do some action?
- If you did, was it the correct action?
- If you didn't take some action, why is that? What stopped you?
- What thoughts from other people impacted you?

What we need to do here is build belief in your why now, so that when you hit hurdles, you will keep on going. Every person who ever had a goal was presented with obstacles. These are mostly thoughts about our own ability. Your mind is your greatest challenge. This is the reason I dedicated a whole chapter to this topic.

Belief starts with your own self-esteem. Self-esteem is really your reputation with yourself. If you believe that you will keep the promises that you make to yourself, then your esteem rises. If you don't, your esteem falls, and your belief in yourself falls with it. Build your self-esteem slowly but steadily (hence Endurance) and keep the promises that you make to yourself. Start small and keep those. For example, if you are not going to buy coffee for a day, then do it. Then build on that.

You have to build self-esteem, which builds belief. Then you will believe yourself when you say that the goal is reachable, attainable. You will believe you can correct course if you go off the rails—there are always hurdles that need to be managed along the way to an end goal.

Think about it like this.

For example, your goal is to get a loan for a house.

One of the checklist items for a bank is to see a record of saving activity. This shows them that you can save and keep monthly repayments going. This will need to be for six months or more, depending on circumstances.

This is your responsibility to complete. The bank can't help you, and it needs to see the activity around this saving plan.

In this example, you start strong. For the first three months, you have saved money to show that you could make repayments. Then your friends indicate that they are going to take a trip somewhere. You don't want to miss out. The only money you have is in the savings account.

This is where your mind starts to act, and you have thoughts like:

- You don't want to miss out on this trip; they might not invite you on the next one.
- You can start the savings again after you come back.
- You weren't likely to make the saving goal anyway, so you should just enjoy yourself.

If you really want the bank loan for a house, and you have strong belief around it, then you could explain the situation to your friends and keep your savings goal going.

To bring this back to wealth creation, you might hit a brick wall where you just want to buy something. It might be something small like a chocolate, or it might be something big like a car. It might be something bigger, like an item of clothing or some shoes. It might be something even bigger in terms of sporting equipment or something like that.

Now you really have to think:

- At that point in time, what is more important?
- Is the new item important, or is your long-term goal?
- Is it a need or a want? Do you actually need it?
- Is it something that is 100 percent required for you to live your life within your goal, or is it a nice-to-have?

To guard against these thoughts, you need to build belief but constantly reaffirm your Reason. You can do this by:

- Using mantras or affirmations
- Creating smaller pictures of your vision you can carry
- Creating a few word cards to evoke the emotions of your vision
- Having a picture on your phone of your vision board (as a background or similar)
- Sticking your Reason up around the house
- Telling others so they help keep you accountable

You're going to have stumbling blocks, and you're going to have things that don't go well, so you need belief in that Reason to keep on going.

Modern-Day Examples

Steve Jobs and Bill Gates saw the power of the computer and wanted to make sure everybody had access to this new power. They wanted to create a computer for everybody but had slightly different views of how to do that. Steve Jobs's vision was more about disrupting the status quo and giving the individual the power of the corporations.

He was trying to level the playing field. Bill Gates wanted to have a PC on everybody's desk. They had similar goals, and they used their vision as a guiding principle in terms of corporate decisions. When making business decisions, the question was: Is this bringing me closer to my goal or taking me further away?

You have people who have a Reason to build for themselves or others. The classic example is Warren Buffett—the most famous investor in the world. Buffett consistently sought out shares trading at 30 percent below their value. If they met that threshold, he would take a deeper interest and conduct further research.

His overarching focus was: Will this provide value for my portfolio, and will it provide value in the long term? He had his objectives for his investments, and if something didn't fit, regardless of what other people thought, he wasn't interested in it.

Look at athletes like Steph Curry, LeBron James, and Michael Jordan when he was younger. They all had a vision of being the best. Not just good, not just making the team—being the best. And that vision drove every single training session, every single game, every single decision about their diet, their sleep, and their training.

Michael Jordan famously highlighted his failures to explain his success, stating: "I've missed more than nine thousand shots in my career. I've lost almost three hundred games. Twenty-six times, I've been trusted to take the game-winning shot and missed. I've failed over and over and over again in my life. And that is why I succeed." But he kept going because his Reason was to be the greatest basketball player of all time. I think he achieved it.

That's the power of having a clear, compelling reason. It keeps you going when things get tough. It helps you make decisions. It guides your actions every single day.

A Mentoring Story

I remember working with a young guy—let's call him Jack—when I was in the UK. Jack was in his early twenties, and he came to me because he felt stuck. He had a decent job, but he felt like he was just going through the motions. Getting up, going to work, coming home, watching TV, going to bed. Repeat.

When I asked him what he wanted out of life, he shrugged. "I don't know. More money, I guess. Maybe a nicer car." But his voice was flat. There was no energy there.

I asked him a different question: "If you could do anything—anything at all—and money wasn't an issue, what would you do?"

He thought for a long time. Then quietly he said, "I've always wanted to build model trains. Like, really intricate ones. Whole landscapes with towns and mountains and tunnels. When I was a kid, my granddad had a setup in his shed, and I used to spend hours there with him. But he died when I was twelve, and...I don't know. I guess I just forgot about it."

Now his voice had energy. His eyes lit up. This was something real.

I said, "Okay, so why don't you do it?"

"Because...I don't know. It seems silly. It's just a hobby. It's not going to make me rich or anything."

"But it makes you happy?"

"Yeah. It does."

We worked together over the next few months. Jack started with a small setup in his spare room. Then he was documenting his builds on social media. People loved it. He received commissions—people wanted him to build custom setups for them. Within a year, he'd quit his job and was running his own business, building custom model train installations for collectors and museums.

The money? It came. But more importantly, Jack had a reason to get up in the morning. He had energy. He had a purpose. He was living his why. That's what a strong Reason can do. It transforms your life from black-and-white to full color, from going through the motions to living with intention.

What's your reason? What makes you light up the way Jackl lit up when he talked about those trains? Find that. Nurture it. Build your life around it. Because that's where the magic happens.

Matthew's Journey

Matthew's journey around his Reason goes over a few sessions. I will break up the commentary with session titles so you can see the conversation evolve.

First Session

After the pleasantries of introduction and basic "getting-to-know-you" have been completed, the coach gets down to business.

MENTOR: Throughout our time together, I will be referring to a framework that I use with my students. It gives our time together some structure and focus. ROGUE defines the five things we will explore on your way to your goal—Reason, Organization, Gratitude, YoU, and Endurance. I'll try and explain things as we go through.

Matthew, have you ever had a goal? Have you ever had a vision? Why do you go to work? What's driving you to work?

MATTHEW: I haven't spent much time thinking about them. I just do it—I mean, my degree and my job. I just fell into it. I left school and went to uni because that's what everyone did. I did some data stuff because I was good at it and then got a job as an analyst. I didn't think much about it. The job's good.

MENTOR: Matthew, what are you here for? I mean, we can use ROGUE for wealth creation. Why do you want to be wealthy?

MATTHEW: I just want some money.

MENTOR: Yes, I understand that, but why? What do you want to do with that? What is your Reason? Why do you want money?

Matthew pauses for a minute.

MATTHEW: I want to travel. I wanted to travel when I was younger and do something that was fun and different.

MENTOR: Okay, all right, that's good. Why do you want to travel? Why is that interesting to you?

MATTHEW: Well, I want to see historical sites. I've always been fascinated by history. I want to see the Roman Empire, Athens, and some of the islands. And I'd love to see the pyramids as well at some stage.

MENTOR: Why do you want to go see those things? What's important about that for you?

MATTHEW: Well, I just enjoyed learning about the evolution of man and some of the things that we've done. I've been fascinated by this, and maybe if we understand them some more, we can learn a little bit more about our own history and maybe what we need to do to stop what's going on now. And also just take the focus off the future and learn from the past. We seem to constantly repeat ourselves.

MENTOR: That's a great start. I think what you need to do now when you go home is to keep going through this process until you really get to the core. There are some questions I'm going to give you to work through. These might help come up with your Reason.

Because wanting money is not going to get you up in the morning. You want to travel, but why? Explore history, but why? Go through the questions here on the sheet, and then next time, we will talk about getting a little deeper.

The questions on the sheet were:

- *If money and time were not important, what would you be doing now?*
- *If you could study anything, what would it be? Why?*

- *What tasks when completed have given you a deep sense of satisfaction?*
- *What activities do you do where you completely lose track of time— ones that you can do for hours on end without exhaustion or frustration?*
- *What would you do for free if you could?*
- *Whom do you like to work with? How do you like to work?*
- *What places, sights, and scenes would you like to see yourself in?*
- *If you were given another twenty-four hours each week, what would you spend it on?*
- *If you were given a million dollars to live on, what would you do with your time?*
- *If you could volunteer in any location for anything, what would it be?*

MATTHEW: Okay, I can go through those.

MENTOR: This is the stuff that we will need to dig into, because this will determine your Reason. This is why you're going to get up in the morning and do hard things to get to your end goal. We will use a principle called the Five Whys. I know we've only just touched on the surface here, but this is where you need to start and ask yourself these questions. And sometimes your Reason will be one thing, or it might be multiple things, or it might be a cascade of things. As you complete one, there's another one, and you already know what that is, but you've outlined the steps.

What we need to do now is put some action around the goal by starting small. All right?

MATTHEW: All right. I'll see how I go.

Second Session

MENTOR: So how did you do with those questions?

MATTHEW: Yes, I did do some work on that.

MENTOR: Okay, great. Let's hear it. And then we will see what the next step is.

MATTHEW: Okay, Reason. We talked about archaeology and the evolution of man. And I found that really, underneath it all, I was fascinated by the human spirit. When the human spirit faces obstacles, it's still amazing what it can do. You look at the Roman Empire and the Greeks. The Greeks were experimenting with democracy long before anyone else even imagined it, while most societies were still governed by city-states and powerful rulers. As the Roman Empire grew, they created such a huge empire by assimilating. Yes, I know they didn't do it all the right way, but they assimilated and made sure that those people that were amazing and had talent were still given the opportunity to display that talent. They created astonishing monuments and architecture because they could harness that. Some of the emperors were awful, but some were really remarkable.

I want to understand the past so that I can positively impact the future. Like most people, I want to do something positive in the world, and sitting here, I'm not doing that. I'm interested in going out there and exploring, while trying to understand the resilience that people showed, and then trying to teach kids resilience because I feel like that's something that's missing today. If I understand what really brought out resilience, then I could create something that I could do to help people of today also build that resilience. That's maybe my Reason: trying to build resilience.

MENTOR: Okay. Those are really some fantastic thoughts. That is a great starting point. I could hear the passion in your voice. I could see you talking to kids. Let's dive a little deeper. Are you okay with that?

MATTHEW: Sure.

MENTOR: We are going to go through the Five Whys. I'm going to start this, and we can see how far we get. You might have to think about the rest between our sessions. Why do you want to teach resilience?

MATTHEW: I think it is something that is missing in people's lives. I see a lot of people getting distracted and missing out on opportunities.

MENTOR: Great. Why do you want to help people remove distractions and get opportunities?

MATTHEW: I think I have missed some, and I can't focus, so I don't want people to have that guilty or negative feeling.

MENTOR: All right. Why do you have a guilty or negative feeling about distractions and opportunities?

MATTHEW: I think I've missed out on things that I regret I did. I wish I could have that time back and do those things. I wish I could get those opportunities back and give them a go. I might be a different person now.

MENTOR: Okay. Why do you want to be a different person?

MATTHEW: I would be more confident and maybe try new things that I would like to. I feel stuck in my work already. But it is interesting, and I like it, but I could be doing so much more.

MENTOR: Why do you feel stuck?

MATTHEW: I can't see my future in front of me. I just see myself stuck to my desk and not growing. I feel like I'm going to be doing this for the rest of my life.

MENTOR: Why do you feel like you will be doing this the rest of your life?

MATTHEW: I won't try things. I don't feel confident. I don't feel I should. I have a good job. I should be happy.

MENTOR: We will stop there. I can hear some emotion in your voice. You were very honest. Sometimes this works, and sometimes it can just drift. The more honest you are, the better the results, and the better the answers and understanding you get. You could keep going if you wanted. You can maybe do that yourself.

What did you learn from this?

MATTHEW: A few things struck a chord with me:

- Even though I'm only twenty-seven, I already feel stuck.
- I lack confidence.
- I don't want others to follow my path.
- I want to try new things.
- I should be happy.

MENTOR: And there were some more, however you need to discover those.

We make decisions at emotional levels and then try to rationalize them. Not the other way around. This is why the Reason has to be an emotional goal. Because if you said, 'I want to make a million dollars this year,' that's not really going to inspire you. It'll inspire you to a point, but it's just a number.

If, however, you want to lead resilience training for youth to make sure that they are set up for life, that's going to get you out of bed every morning. That's going to get you out of there. It's based on something you want for yourself as well and it has emotional pull.

MATTHEW: That makes sense. I did feel the emotion as I spoke.

MENTOR: I'm sure you did. The next thing is starting to make this Reason more tangible to see, hear. Do you like to see things? Hear things?

MATTHEW: Sorry, what?

MENTOR: I don't think I said that right. Out of these three options, what makes the most sense to you. If your partner:

1. Looked you in the eyes and said, "I love you."
2. Gave you a present as she said, "I love you."
3. Gave you a big hug while she said, "I love you."

MATTHEW: The third option. I need to feel her arms around me while she said it. I would believe her then.

MENTOR: That means you are about the feeling something gives. The sensations of the senses at the same time as the words. The words by themselves aren't enough. It makes sense—the present you probably don't think you are worthy of, based on what you have said. I would agree with that.

MATTHEW: I suppose.

MENTOR: For next time, I want you to keep going on exploring your Reason. Take the other answers that you came up with from the questions and ask why. Ask why till you start saying the same things. See what other thoughts of feelings come up.

I also want you to start writing out the feelings, sensations that you will feel when you help the kids. What are you seeing, smelling, and hearing? How do you feel when a kid gets what you are trying to teach? Or the kid (or parents) thank you for your help and really mean it?

MATTHEW: I can do that.

Third Session

MENTOR: Okay, let's continue with your Reason and the few homework exercises from last week. They were asking whys of your other answers and then trying to get some sensations around the Reason.

MATTHEW: Yes, I did that. The whys were similar. I got to similar places but only slightly nuanced.

MENTOR: That makes sense. Normally something is part of us or not. That seems quite central to you.

MATTHEW: I also tried to get some words for how I would feel, but I struggled with that. I couldn't really feel it.

MENTOR: Okay. Let's try something else. You have two options that I suggest:

1. Do a day in the life of your new Reason. Think about your Reason coming true. What would a typical day look like? Pick a day when you might be working with the kids. What are you seeing? How is the day going? At the end of the day, what are you feeling?

2. Or you can pick a time in the future. Let's look ten years ahead. It seems fair. What are you doing at that point in time? What have you done? What are you working toward? How are you now enacting that goal? I want you to get really deep and make it come alive for you. Do whatever you want to bring that alive and then start to really picture yourself doing that.

Think about which might work for you. Don't rationalize; just make notes and write whenever comes to mind. It can't be right or wrong. They are just feelings.

MATTHEW: I can do that.

MENTOR: Once we have this, the next step is building belief and a feeling of responsibility for this goal of yours.

MATTHEW: Why are we doing this?

MENTOR: What we are doing is creating a vision of the future to inspire and drive you forward. We didn't want to have something simple or basic like "I want to buy a house." You'll probably do that naturally. It's not something inspiring. However, creating a program about resilience and trying to teach that to others—well, that's big. That's why you're building wealth.

Every time when you start to do things, you can say to yourself, "OK, is this going to build my wealth? Because my wealth is going to allow me to teach resilience." That building block then allows you to continue to say, "I'm not trying to deny myself; I just realize that this is not helping me toward my goal." That's what this is all about.

Wealth creation, which is what I'm here to help you with, is really about the simple steps. It's letting time be your leverage. It's about starting small and building up.

MATTHEW: I can understand that.

MENTOR: Next time, we will talk about building belief.

Fourth Session

MENTOR: How did you go with your Reason exercise?

MATTHEW: Good. I got some good thoughts down on paper. They made sense.

MENTOR: It is interesting that it has to make sense to you. You say that a lot.

MATTHEW: So?

MENTOR: This is really about the two parts of you. You did the personality test and have two parts of you (see chapter 2: "YoU")—Blue and Yellow. And sense can link to both of those personalities. Blue—logic. Yellow—feelings and the five senses.This is starting to link up correctly.

MATTHEW: Okay. I can see that.

MENTOR: The next stage now is building belief. To do that, you need to take your thoughts. Which did you do—day in the life or ten years from now?

MATTHEW: Day in the life.

MENTOR: You need to take the thoughts from that exercise and make it come alive. You could do this in a few ways that would work for you:

1. You could make a recording of it so you can listen to it.
2. You can create a vision board but with some feeling words on it.

You need to make the choice.

MATTHEW: The vision board sounds right.

MENTOR: Okay. Grab pictures, words—mostly feeling words—and give your thoughts the vision you were describing. Create that day in pictures. Let your imagination take the reins and create how best to see it. Do it once. Look at it; review it. If it is not right, do it again. Do it until you really see yourself in that place.

This is your Reason. This is what is going to help you build wealth as well as the life you want once you have wealth.

MATTHEW: Sounds exciting.

MENTOR: Great. I'm glad you think so. The next step is building the belief. You are going to have times when things get tough or people question what you are doing.

MATTHEW: Yeah, I've already seen that. One of my mates at work keeps saying, "Why do you bring your lunch to work? This is not the playground," trying to make me feel small and stuff. The first couple of times, I've been able to shrug him off, and that's been okay. But yeah, it might get a little bit more difficult in the future.

MENTOR: That's exactly what I'm talking about. People want to pull you back to where they are because that's where they're comfortable. He's probably a good friend. He doesn't want to lose you. He doesn't want to be left behind. You could try talking to him about what you're trying to do. He might understand; he might be supportive. But sometimes you also find some friends just fall by the wayside because they're not aligned with you and they hold you back.

Those are difficult choices because they test you as a person and your goal, your Reason, what's important to you. And this is where people start to struggle. This is where belief will be so important.

MATTHEW: How do I build belief?

MENTOR: The main way is continuing looking at your vision board—at least once a week—and feeling the feelings. Seeing that day and similar days like it. Make it so much a part of you that you don't want to *not* do it. I know that sounds simple. It is, but it is also very powerful. Here are some powerful quotes from some people that might help with this:

- "Believe you can and you're halfway there."—Theodore Roosevelt
- "Don't let the noise of others' opinions drown out your own inner voice."—Steve Jobs
- "You can have anything you want if you are willing to give up the belief that you can't have it."—Robert Anthony

There are many more. And they all say similar things.

MATTHEW: I'll give it a go.

MENTOR: This will be one of the hardest things you will do, building belief in yourself, but it will be one of the most rewarding. I will also help you through this as much as I can.

Your Turn

Now it is your turn to start to work on creating your Reason.

Find a quiet place and give yourself an hour to start this exercise. Get some pens, paper, magazines, a laptop, your phone, books, whatever you think you might need.

Ask yourself the following questions (as stated above) and then go into the Five Whys:

1. If money and time were not important, what would you be doing now?
2. If you could study anything, what would it be? Why?
3. What tasks when completed have given you a deep sense of satisfaction?
4. What activities do you do where you completely lose track of time, ones that you can do for hours on end without exhaustion or frustration?
5. What would you do for free if you could?
6. Whom do you like to work with? How do you like to work?
7. What places, sights, and scenes would you like to see yourself in?
8. If you were given another twenty-four hours each week, what would you spend it on?
9. If you were given a million dollars to live on, what would you do with your time?
10. If you could volunteer in any location for anything, what would it be?

Once you have your answers, allow yourself to sit with them for a week.

Look back at them often to edit, add, refine, and clarify.

Once you have something that feels right, select a method to help bring the Reason to life. Do one or do all. Get the tools and start to make the Reason real.

Keep refining it until it makes sense and looks, reads, and sounds like you want it to. This is your Reason that will keep you going. This isn't the end of it, but it is a good starting point toward achieving that Reason.

Notes

Notes

Notes

CHAPTER 2
ORGANIZATION

You will never change your life until you change something you do daily. The secret of your success is found in your daily routine.

—Matthew C. Maxwell

This is where the hard work starts. Everything that is worthwhile requires effort. But we need to be smart about the work and make sure it is done correctly. This chapter is about getting yourself moving and working toward your Reason. There are many things we can do to get ourselves going, and I have listed the ones that have worked for me and others. I also talk about habits—such a key driver of helping achieve your Reason. The right habits help; the wrong ones hinder.

My Story

Once I had my Reason, I needed to figure out how to actually get there. Having a dream is one thing, but making it happen is another. That's where Organization comes in—the O in ROGUE.

I didn't have much financial knowledge when I started. I had just finished university, had no money saved, and didn't really understand investments. I knew I needed to learn, so my first action was to seek out information.

I started going to seminars. The first ones I attended were about property investment because that's what my parents had done. I bought some books about share investing. But then I realized I'd jumped too far ahead—I didn't actually understand the basics of wealth creation itself. That's when I discovered two books that transformed my thinking.

The first was *Rich Dad, Poor Dad*, by Robert Kiyosaki.[6] That book got me thinking about wealth creation in a very different way. It talked about the first steps of savings, understanding jargon, and the difference between assets and liabilities. It emphasized that you're not going to have investments straightaway. It also explained balance sheets, loans, repayments, debt, and all of these other financial terms that I'd started to hear but didn't really understand. It clarified the jargon.

The second book that I found extremely useful was *The Richest Man in Babylon*, by George S. Clason.[7] It was written in 1926, and it's still going strong. It's written as a parable and talks about Babylon as the most prosperous city of its time nearly four thousand years ago. It's about people in that city and how they accumulated their wealth. It opened my eyes to the simple fundamentals of wealth creation.

First, put aside a little bit of money that you keep for yourself. You may say, "All the money I earn is for myself." However, most goes toward bills, expenses, and mortgages. The book indicated that we need to keep something back for ourselves to invest and grow. The author talks about keeping some money to invest in yourself. There are many ways this can be done, for example:

---

6 *Rich Dad, Poor Dad*—Robert Kiyosaki (1997)

7 *he Richest Man in Babylon*—George S. Clason (1926)

- The first 10 percent of money earned is kept for investment.
- The 50/30/20 rule—where 20 percent is kept for debt repayment and investment, 50 percent for living expenses (needs), and 30 percent is for other expenses (wants).
- The 10/10/80 rule—where 10 percent is kept for investment, 10 percent is for debt reduction, and the remaining 80 percent is for living expenses (both needs and wants).

In each of these examples (and there are others), money is put aside for your future and put to work for you in investments; the rest is to use to live now.

Second, the only way that you can create wealth is if your spending is less than your income. I know this isn't a radical thought, but we have lots of little voices and thoughts that say, *You could have this; you could have that.* And suddenly our spending goes beyond our means.

I did not grow up with lots of money. I didn't have a job in my teens, so I didn't have many spending habits. My university days were spent living within my means. After graduating, I got a job and started to have money. I had read these books and also had the voice of my father in my head; I still didn't spend beyond my means.

I had seen my parents write down their spending in a large notebook. Each receipt was put in there, and at the end of the month, a tally was made and compared to their income. I started to do this in a simpler way. I got the money for the week out of the bank. This is what I had to spend. Once it was gone, it was gone. I had to plan my spending to make sure I had the money for the things that were important.

As I grew older and started getting more money, I was very conscious of my spending. I've been astute about tracking my expenses. Once a month, I'd get all my receipts and put them in a book. Later, once Excel existed, I put them into a spreadsheet (does that show my age?), and looked at how much I earned and what I'd spent it on. Then I'd categorize the expenditure.

I'd also put money aside each month so that the money I saved was working for me through shares or other investments (but more on that later).

A lot of this wealth-creation knowledge came out of *Rich Dad, Poor Dad* and *The Richest Man in Babylon*. Beyond books, I attended seminars that talked about debt and savings. I soaked in as much knowledge as I could.

I wanted to build a mindset where I had control of my money and it was working for me. I didn't want to have money control me, or more correctly, have the lack of money control me and what I could do. I was going to control what I did with money so that I could not only live now but also live in the future. By this I mean I wanted to have a choice in the future about what I wanted to do, not just continue to work.

The next stage was: *I need to have my money work for me.* Having my money sitting in a bank account is a good start, but it needs to work harder. I needed to look for other investment choices. So I went to seminars and read books on property and shares. I constantly craved information and knowledge so that I could understand what I was doing and make better and more informed decisions.

The biggest thing I did was start as soon as I could. I didn't wait for the perfect time. I started. Compounding needs time to have the greatest impact.

"Compounding" is a financial phenomenon that makes time work in your favor. It's what happens when your investment earnings are added to your principal, forming a larger base on which earnings may accumulate. And as your investment base gets larger, it has the potential to grow faster.

For all these ideas, you need to understand what you are trying to achieve, and then you have to work them into your daily habits to make them stick. Habits will make the continued work easier to do because it will become automatic.

Habits

Habits are the things that define you. You have your values, attitudes, morals, ethics—all of those things are part of you. But your habits are what you are, what you do, and how you react.

Habits are those things that allow us to function and allow the subconscious to take over and just do the things that we have taught it to do. As explained in *The Power of Habit*,[8] there are really three parts to a habit: the trigger, the action, and then the reward.

The easiest example is brushing your teeth. The trigger is you go to your bathroom, probably after breakfast sometime, before you set off for work. You pick up the toothbrush. You put toothpaste on the toothbrush. You stick the toothbrush in your mouth in the same spot you do every day. And you do the same brushing every day.

It's either what you were taught as a kid or what you learned was important. And you brush your teeth the same way each time. Sometimes, it's a little bit longer, sometimes a little shorter, but a lot of the other stuff is just a habit that you have formed. Then you'll

8 *The Power of Habits*—Charles Duhigg

spit out, rinse out, wipe your mouth—whatever you do, however you do it, it'll be the same.

As an exercise, maybe tomorrow after you've read this, consciously stick your toothbrush somewhere else in your mouth. If you normally start on the left, start on the right. You'll find that it feels awkward, and naturally you'll put the toothbrush back on the other side and go through your routine. You will not be able to easily change that.

Those sorts of habits are "good." You don't need to consciously be aware of how you clean your teeth or in what order. You have created a habit that ensures each tooth will be brushed.

There are three parts to a habit—this has been proven in many scientific papers and been written about in many personal development books as well[9]. The three parts are:

1. The Trigger
    a. This is the circumstance that starts the habit. From the tooth-brushing example, it is stepping into the bathroom after breakfast.
2. The Routine/Action
    b. This is the process that we do automatically. From the tooth-brushing example, it is the process of actually brushing the teeth.
3. The Reward
    c. This is the signal that we have completed the process. From the tooth-brushing example, it is the clean-teeth feel.

---

9 The Power of Habits-Charles Duhrigg

Graybiel AM. *The basal ganglia and chunking of action repertoires.* Neurobiol Learn Mem. 1998 Jul-Sep;70(1-2):119-36. doi: 10.1006/nlme.1998.3843. PMID: 9753592.

A. David Smith, J. Paul Bolam, *The neural network of the basal ganglia as revealed by the study of synaptic connections of identified neurones*, Trends in Neurosciences, V13, I7,1990 (259-265), ISSN 0166-2236,https://doi.org/10.1016/0166-2236(90)90106-K.

There are different thoughts on how long a habit takes to be called "a habit." However, it is generally agreed that you need to do something for at least three months before it will become a habit. That is quite a long time.

Our day is filled with habits.

We have a get-up-in-the-morning habit. We have a rushing-teeth-and-getting-ready-for-work habit. We have a breakfast habit. We have a driving-to-work habit. We have a morning-break habit. We have a lunch habit. We have an afternoon habit. If you really wanted to, you could go through a full day without engaging your brain at all because your subconscious will take care of everything for you.

Habits can be good, bad, or indifferent. In terms of health, good habits might be going to the gym or eating a salad for lunch or walking to work or taking the stairs. They're still just habits, but they're probably seen as good ones. Some so-called "bad" habits might be buying an afternoon snack from the vending machine, having three or four coffees in the morning, or getting takeout on the way home because you can't be bothered with cooking. These would be considered "bad" habits if your goal is to be very healthy.

Then there are neutral habits, like brushing your teeth or combing your hair. They don't have a major impact—they're just habits that we have. They save us time and allow our brains to do more important things.

But what we're really interested in here are your financial habits. Sometimes we don't even know we have financial habits. Like all habits, they exist, but we might not be conscious of them until we actually slow down and consciously participate in our lives and decisions.

There are many different financial habits. Here are some examples people have:

- Spending any money in their bank account.
- Giving to a charity person every time they walk past them.
- Buying a weekly train ticket on Monday.
- Going to the bottle shop on Friday to get a six-pack.
- Going out for lunch every Sunday.
- Buying a coffee every day before work.
- Putting every $2 coin they get in a container for the bank.
- Rounding up their bill and giving the rest to charity or as a tip.

There are many others. The more important question is: How many are you aware of?

All of these habits add up. They can impact our ability to plan for our current circumstances and also to build for our future.

What do we need to do here?

1. Write down our financial habits when they happen.
2. Be aware of them and make conscious decisions to either do them or not do them.
3. Don't criticize them; just analyze them to understand where they come from.
4. Continue to have awareness about them.
5. Understand the three parts of the habit—trigger, routine, reward.
   a. Why does it happen?
   b. Are you bored?
   c. Are you hungry?

d. Are you needing a break?
e. Are you wanting a social connection?

Here's a habit example: At 3:00 p.m., you go down to the cafeteria and get a coffee. Or you go to the kitchen area and make yourself a tea, and you always get something from the vending machine. Whatever it is doesn't matter. You're not judging yourself. You are understanding where you're at.

Table 1: Cost of Coffee: One Coffee per Day for Each Day of the Week

Cost of Cup of Coffee	Weekly Cost (7 days)	Monthly Cost (30 days)	Yearly Cost
$4.50	$31.50	$135	$1,642.50
$5.50	$38.50	$165	$2.007.50
$6.50	$45.50	$195	$2,372.50

If we use this coffee example, the above table explains a little about the impact on your finances of that one purchase. Depending on the cost of an individual cup and how many you have in a day, you could be spending over $2,000 a year on coffee alone. If you have more than one cup, possibly two cups—one as you get to work and then one later in the morning—it could cost you $4,000 per year.

Later, in the chapter on Endurance, I look at how this (the money spent on coffee) might be used to start your compounding investments.

Charles Duhigg in *The Power of Habit* goes through this process of understanding your habits. He has a really excellent example about the afternoon snack. He notices that at 3:00 p.m., he goes for a walk, goes to the cafeteria, and buys a cookie. He's noticed over time that he's put on some weight. He's trying to understand why he does this. After a few weeks of working through that habit, he realizes that he's actually after social connection. He wants to have a little bit of a break and connect with somebody in the middle of the workday. It's not a big thing, but that's what he's really after. Not the cookie.

So he changes that habit to look for social connection rather than the cookie in the cafeteria. And that's why you need to understand what your habit is.

This is especially true for your financial habits. If you see money in the bank and you feel the urge to spend it, there are ways to get around that. You just move that money into a different account so you don't see it, and so you don't spend it.

Have good habits and understand your bad habits, then make sure that the bad ones are changed or mitigated and the good ones are emphasized.

If we understand our habits, we can create new ones to help reach our financial goals. Here are a few examples of "good" financial habits to make wealth creation a habit:

- Create a saving plan that needs no input from you—a monthly withdrawal to another account.
- Bring your coffee or lunch to work.
- Take a list when you go shopping.
- Investigate different utilities companies to get the best deal.
- Before each purchase, stop and ask: Do I really need this?
- Don't link automatic payment methods to online shopping.

- Don't use debt to buy things (such as Afterpay, credit cards, etcetera).
- Pay off your credit card as you use it.
- Sell unused items on eBay or Facebook to make some extra cash.
- Keep a record of your spending.

There are many others. In the next section we are going to look into detail on a few of these.

How Do We Begin Using Habits to Create Wealth?

How do you start creating wealth? As I mentioned in the beginning, people think it is about shares or property or other investment vehicles, but really it starts much earlier than that.

Tracking

Understand how you spend your money. In today's world, it is easy to track and know where your money is going. Most banking apps have built-in cash flow trackers. These let you see what you are spending and where. It helps you categorize your spending into buckets, making it easy to see where most of your money goes. This is always the first step. Once you know this, then you can make changes if you need to.

If you don't like technology, then you can do it the old-fashioned way and buy yourself a little notebook and write down each expense. Later on, you can put it into Excel or in a different book to track totals.

Table 2: A Sample Tracking Sheet

Year	Month	Mortgage / Rent	Holiday	Car	Eating Out	General Household	Groceries	Health	Utilities	Insurance	Telco	School	Total	Saving	Income	Difference
20XX	1	$ 1,950		$ 76	$ 398	$ 1,498	$ 1,053	$ 245		$ 147	$ 325		$ 5,692	$ 250	$ 6,667	$ 725
20XX	2	$ 1,950		$ 80	$ 737	$ 256	$ 774	$ 245	$ 664	$ 147	$ 325	$ 50	$ 4,728	$ 250	$ 6,667	$ 1,688
20XX	3	$ 1,950		$ 95	$ 208	$ 413	$ 1,232	$ 245		$ 147	$ 325		$ 4,616	$ 250	$ 6.667	$ 1,801
20XX	4	$ 1,950		$ 65	$ 124	$ 869	$ 1,018	$ 245		$ 147	$ 325	$ 50	$ 4,793	$ 250	$ 6,667	$ 1,623
20XX	5	$ 1,950		$ 450	$ 317	$ 1,815	$ 1,072	$ 245	$ 845	$ 747	$ 325		$ 7,766	$ 250	$ 6,667	-$ 1,349
20XX	6	$ 1,950	$1,395	$ 250	$ 122	$ 306	$ 1,060	$ 245	$ 166	$ 147	$ 325		$ 5,966	$ 250	$ 6,667	$ 451
20XX	7	$ 1,950		$ 80	$ 377	$ 975	$ 827	$ 245		$ 147	$ 325	$ 50	$ 4,976	$ 250	$ 6,667	$ 1,441
20XX	8	$ 1,950		$ 65	$ 49	$ 101	$ 1,274	$ 245	$ 703	$ 147	$ 325		$ 4,858	$ 250	$ 6,667	$ 1,558
20XX	9	$ 1,950		$ 75	$ 426	$ 344	$ 1,125	$ 245	$ 686	$ 147	$ 325		$ 5,323	$ 250	$ 6.667	$ 1,094
20XX	10	$ 1,950		$ 230	$ 60	$ 692	$ 868	$ 245		$ 147	$ 325	$ 50	$ 4,567	$ 250	$ 6,667	$ 1,850
20XX	11	$ 1,950		$ 80	$ 234	$ 1,529	$ 1,134	$ 245	$ 438	$ 147	$ 325		$ 6,082	$ 250	$ 6.667	$ 334
20XX	12	$ 1,950	$3.520	$ 86	$ 270	$ 1,157	$ 1,049	$ 245	$1.821	$ 147	$ 325		$10,569	$ 250	$ 6.667	-$ 4,153
Totals		$ 23,400	$4.915	$1,632	$ 2,822	$ 9,957	$12,465	$2,940	$5,322	$ 2,364	$3.900	$ 200	$69,936	$3,000	$80,000	$ 7,064

Then you can see what is going on. Using the example spreadsheet above, you could ask yourself a few questions, such as:

- Do I need so much health insurance? Is there a better deal?
- Why is spending higher in December than other months? Can I do something about this, like open a Christmas saver account?
- Do I actually have $7,000 left in my account each year? If not, where is the rest going? What money haven't I accounted for?
- Why is there such a difference in my monthly expenses on General Household?
- Can I smooth out[10] my bill payments on my utilities?
- What do I get for $325 per month for my phone bill? Is that needed?

You can see that once you have this information, you can then investigate your spending habits and work out how to improve.

10 Bill smoothing is a payment arrangement that divides your estimated annual energy (electricity or gas) costs into equal, regular installments—weekly, fortnightly, or monthly—rather than requiring large quarterly payments. It helps with household budgeting, avoids "bill shock" from high seasonal usage, and usually involves direct debit.

Saving

The goal of saving is to get started with whatever amount you have, whether it's $5, $10 or $100. This doesn't sound like much, but it starts a new habit. one that, if it continues, will get you on the road to your wealth dreams. How do you go about this?

1. Open a new cardless bank account—one with a higher interest rate.
2. Create a direct debit from your normal account to your new savings account each month for the amount you want to save.
3. After a certain saving level, put the money into something else that will provide you with higher returns.

Putting your savings into another account with no card access means you can't access the money by tap or card or online shopping. This also means you don't need to actively do anything each month, and you don't "see" it. You are already starting on your wealth journey.

How does this help? It is not about the amount; it is about the habit and putting money aside for yourself and your future. It is investing in yourself first, which can be a big mind shift for those who normally put everyone else first. Pay the bills, pay my debts, pay the groceries. All these things are important, but are you not important as well? This is why you need to pay yourself first through saving.

For example, if you are paid $1,000, then $100 goes to yourself into your savings account. Then $100 goes toward your debts—on top of what you already pay. And the remaining $800 is for your day-to-day expenses—food, rent, car, utilities, whatever.

This last part might be a shock when you are used to having $1,000 for your expenses. However, it is amazing how resourceful people can be when they know there is a future they are saving for. This is why your Reason is so important and needs to be big. If you have that out in front of you, you know why you are doing this and will make it happen.

Financial Rituals and Routines

To harness the power of Organization and also to start your wealth journey, focus on three key areas:

1. **Establish clear routines to help overcome temptations.**
    a. Start your day, begin your work, and wind down with a consistent routine.
        - For example, get up slightly earlier to make your lunch and brew your own coffee; go for a morning run rather than spend money on a gym membership that you only use occasionally.

    b. In the evening, we are at our weakest (willpower-wise), so don't make it easy to break good routines.
        - For example, if you exercise in the evening, have your gym or running clothes out, depending on whether you need your gym membership. Plan your meals so you don't get stuck just getting takeaway. Get good rest to start your next day fresh.
2. **Prioritize effectively.**
    a. You have a Reason. Make sure you use that as a guide to help do things during your week or month. Regularly ask yourself, "What can I do to move myself forward

in my goal to wealth creation?" This helps concentrate your efforts on what truly matters. This should link back to your Reason.

b. For example, what books can you read to get more knowledge on investments? Can you analyze your spending habits more to get further insights? Whom can I talk to to help me on my journey?

3. **Keep Evaluating Your Habits.**

a. As mentioned previously, continue to explore your habits. New ones will start to emerge; make sure that they are ones that bring you closer or align to your wealth creation goal.

Time Management

Understanding the value of time is another critical aspect of organization. You may be able to create more wealth, but unfortunately, we cannot create more time, so we need to guard it and use it wisely. We have 1,440 minutes in a day, and roughly 42,573,600 minutes in a lifetime. Efficient use of this finite resource is essential for reaching your goals.

On an average day, after accounting for sleep, meals, and basic necessities, we are left with about 780 minutes. How you utilize this time determines your productivity and progress toward your Reason or your wealth-creation goal. It's important to recognize that everyday tasks and distractions, like doing chores or checking email, can fragment your focus and steal valuable time to be able to help you move forward.

To maximize your use of time for your wealth creation, think about using the following two strategies:

1. **Time blocking.** Allocate specific hours for focused, uninterrupted work. Start with two-hour blocks and gradually increase to three hours as you build endurance. This practice enhances your ability to concentrate deeply on your most important tasks.
    a. This might be used for reading or investing different investment options. It might be used to determine the best savings account or how to analyze your spending. This might be time spent on study—both formal and informal.
2. **Eliminate distractions.** Identify and remove distractions—be they social media, phone notifications, or external interruptions. Create an environment that fosters concentration and eliminates disruptions.
    b. Shut down or remove accounts that you don't need. Tell people what you are doing and when you will be finished so you don't get needless interruptions.

By organizing your time and habits effectively, you unlock your potential to achieve incredible results. Embrace these practices, and you'll be amazed at what you can accomplish.

Find the Right Experts

You can't do everything alone. Getting help in key areas will drastically speed up your progress and means you can focus on your area of expertise. This is not a reflection on you or your skills; it is about leveraging your time.

On your wealth-creation journey, you might want to access accountants, financial planners, mortgage specialists, tax consultants, solicitors or conveyancers, or even coaches. There is no time like the present to start to build your network of expertise around you. You can't learn everything there is to know.

You don't need to find all these people now; however, building a network early means that the right people will be around when you need them. Sometimes, when you discover one connection or expert, they may introduce you to colleagues who can assist in other areas.

And remember, when you find these people, *listen.*

Remember the reason you went to find them: for their expertise. You don't need to show them that you know as much as them. They are there for you to tap into their expertise and experience, to help with the areas that you don't know.

You don't just need to look for people with expertise; you can also look for people on the same or similar journey as yourself. Having support from like-minded people can make a difference when things get tough or you feel resistance from people around you. Having someone else to spur you on can be the difference between getting to your goal or falling by the wayside.

Debt

Good debt puts money in your pocket. Bad debt takes it out.

—Robert Kiyosaki

You can't talk about wealth without talking about debt. For most people, debt is one of their biggest fears in their financial journey—and it's often tied to a fear of loss. But debt itself isn't the enemy. The key is understanding the difference between good debt and bad debt.

Good debt builds wealth. It's the kind of debt that helps you buy or create an income-producing asset—a property, a business, or an investment. It's debt that works for you. In Australia and the UK, the interest on these types of debts can often be offset against the income they generate, which makes them powerful tools when used well.

Bad debt, on the other hand, drains your wealth. It's the kind of debt that buys things that lose value—such as cars, gadgets, or furniture. I always smile when people call their car an "asset." Unless you're renting it out, it's not an asset. It's a liability. Every mile (or kilometer) you drive, every service, every tank of gas (or petrol)—they all cost you.

So ask yourself: "Is this debt putting money in my pocket or taking it out?" That one question can change how you see your entire financial picture. I provide an example of how to get out of debt in the story with Matthew below.

Work with a good accountant. Learn how to structure your debt so it serves your long-term goals, not your short-term impulses. When used wisely, debt can be one of your most effective tools for building wealth—and when feared blindly, it becomes your biggest roadblock.

Matthew's Journey

As with Matthew's journey with Reason, his steps through Organization will also continue across multiple sessions. We will split each part by the session and describe what is talked about for Organization each time.

First Session

MENTOR: Now we move onto Organization. Organization is about getting an understanding about yourself and your current situation and then setting up habits and routines to help you get to your goals. Since we are trying to build your wealth, we need to understand your money situation at the moment.

You need to understand your baseline so you know where you need to go from here. Do you have a budget or at least know your spending?

MATTHEW: No, not really. I just work off my balance. If there is money in my account, then I can spend it; if there isn't, then normally I don't. I don't borrow money off others, as I normally struggle to pay them back.

MENTOR: Fair enough. Right, the first thing I want you to do is understand your money spending habits. I don't want you to create a budget in terms of writing out spending limits. I have found that people struggle with that. Instead, I want you to do it in reverse.

MATTHEW: What do you mean?

MENTOR: For the next month, just go about your normal life and buy your everyday things as you normally would. You can either keep all the receipts or use the app that comes with most online banking services these days.

MATTHEW: Yeah, I think I saw that on my banking app.

MENTOR: Don't change your spending; just keep track of it all. What you spend, where you spent it, how much, and whether it was card, cash, online shopping, whatever it was, just so that we know how you spent that money. And then at the end of the month, we'll put it into categories, and we'll work out where you spend your money. Ever done that before?

MATTHEW: No, not really. Sounds tough.

MENTOR: Not with the app. This is the first step. Then we are going to do some budgeting, but in reverse. You'll find naturally that you will be interested in what you are spending and then start to think of why. Don't change anything yet.

MATTHEW: Why would I change anything?

MENTOR: Because as soon as you bring something into focus, you start to change it. It's human nature.

Second Session

MATTHEW: Here's my list of expenses and what I've been doing. I'm not sure what you want to do with this. I've looked through it but didn't do too much otherwise.

MENTOR: What jumped out at you as you looked at it?

MATTHEW: Um, well, I did have a look at some of the categories that were allocated by my app. I couldn't believe that I spent so much on eating out.

MENTOR: Yeah, that's normal. Something always jumps out.

MATTHEW: Also, I seem to spend a lot of money at a gym store, and I don't know what that's about or what I'm doing there.

MENTOR: Okay, that's good. That's well done. Anything else?

MATTHEW: No.

MENTOR: What I want you to do now is go through the budget and do a little bit more of a deep dive on your categories. For the next month, week by week, I want you to look at each of the categories and analyze them a little more. Can you do that?

MATTHEW: Well, yes. I'm a data analyst, so I should be able to do that.

MENTOR: Make categories that make sense to you. I normally use some of the following:

- House
- Car
- Household
- Entertainment
- Debt repayment (if any)
- Groceries
- Alcohol
- Gaming
- Utilities (other than house ones)
- Savings
- Investments
- Pets
- Insurance
- Health
- Pharmacy
- Holidays
- Eating Out

- Study
- Other

You might have some others that you want to track. This is your spending sheet. I just put "Other" for any other expenses. You might see some regular ones you want to track.

Review it week by week, at least at first, and see what those numbers are. See how they line up with your income as well. Is there money left over? Are you spending it all? Are you spending too much? This is the first thing I want you to do.

After that, work out the percentages of each category each week. The baseline for the percentage should be your income. For example, if your income for the week was $1,000, then everything should be as a percentage of the $1,000 (e.g., spend $135 on groceries, then that's 13.5 percent of your income).

Do this for a month. Does anything change week to week? Does anything stay consistent? Are there items that you spend more than you think? Many times, this will give you a really good sense of when, on what, and where you're spending your money. Ask yourself some questions:

- Are you happy spending that percentage of your income on each category?
- Does anything change week to week?
- Does anything stay consistent?
- Are there items that you spend more than you think?

MATTHEW: Got it.

MENTOR: How much are you saving or putting away for investments right now? Because wealth creation starts with savings.

MATTHEW: I think over the month, I saved maybe $50, and I had that down to spend on a new game.

MENTOR: Okay. No dramas.

MATTHEW: I would like to have some savings. My partner and I have talked briefly about buying a house. It doesn't get anywhere.

MENTOR: As you go through this process, you need to write those things down. Those things become important. Why haven't you saved then?

MATTHEW: Never had enough money to. I've got debts to service as well.

MENTOR: What are you doing to get more money?

MATTHEW: Maybe a promotion?

MENTOR: You don't sound too sure. Let's work on the spending, and then next time, we will start on the saving.

Third Session

MENTOR: Let's loop back to your spending. What did you come up with?

MATTHEW: Well, this was easy. This is in my field. I got some spreadsheets and graphs to show you. I found out that about 40 percent of my wage goes on household bills and rent. I spend about another 15 percent on groceries. There's about 15 percent on my car. This month I had to pay some insurance, and I got some new tires as well, so it might have been a little bit more than normal.

I spent 20 percent on going out, which surprised me. I didn't realize I spent that much. I didn't realize I spent so much on gambling, and that's just to have some fun. I spend a lot of money on my gym membership and stuff to do with the gym. That was another 10 percent, which was a lot.

MENTOR: That's great. Did anything surprise you in each of those categories, or was there anything there that you weren't previously aware that you were spending this much on?

MATTHEW: Yeah, well, I didn't realize that I wasn't saving anything. My savings was incidental. I think over the month I saved about $20. And then that was gone the next month. I didn't realize I spent so much on lunches. I thought I took my lunch quite frequently. That was a bit of a shock. And I didn't realize that my gym membership was as high as it was. When I first got it, it was maybe $20 bucks a month. But it's now over $50. I don't know what happened there. That was a surprise.

Then in the third week of the month, my electricity bill came out of my account. That just used up all my savings from the previous weeks. I might have to check if there is a cheaper energy provider. I didn't realize it was that high. Debts repayments were also high but not too much—they came in at 6.5 percent.

MENTOR: This is really good. Having a budget brings awareness. Awareness then creates questions, which turn into action. You have already mentioned some. You'll see that this stuff is not rocket science. We can do something about those debts next week. What else?

MATTHEW: Well, there are a couple of things that I'm going to do. As I said, I'm going to have a look at my energy plans and see if I can get a better one. I thought I'd do this for my mobile as well. See if I can get some better plans based on my usage.

I was then going to go and have a look at different gyms in the area and see if there's a cheaper gym. Or maybe just go for a run in the park.

Then lunch. It seems like I eat out for lunch about three times a week, or I bring my lunch in and go out anyway. Wasting money another way. I think I bring lunch in on Mondays, but then I know we have team lunches that day sometimes. I'm not organized. I think I'm going to change that around to make better use of my groceries, since I realized I do throw a lot away. That'll probably save me a little bit.

The other thing is the gambling. I just don't know why I do that, and I didn't know it was that much. I'm going to try and stop that. I mean, I'll stop that. I'll watch somebody else do it, and I'll get into their excitement, but I'm just not going to do it myself. I'd probably save about $50 a month there.

MENTOR: If you did all those things, how much money do you think you could save yourself?

MATTHEW: Well, if I look at it, lunches are about $20 a pop. I'd still do lunches twice a week, but there's two lunches I'm saving. That's $40 a week. That's possibly $160 a month. If I don't do the pokies, that's another $50-ish. That's $190.

Maybe on the telephone and gas, I could save about $10 a month. I think I should be able to do that. I could save close to $210 to $220 total.

MENTOR: Then let's start saving. First of all, I want you to open a new savings account for yourself. I want you to shut down access to it. No withdrawals allowed in any shape or form. Make it hard to get into and get money out of. Don't link it to any card or allow tap.

I want you to put $250 in that account each month. It seems like you're going to get close to that, but not quite maybe. This will just be a little stretch goal to get some money saved.

When your pay comes in, I want you to put that $250 into the account per month. Then adjust your living expenses to the rest. Do all the other things that you've mentioned. Keep watching and writing out your expenses and see what else you can find. Later on we'll probably up that $250 per month. But right now I just want you to make it simple on yourself. Do you think you can do that?

MATTHEW: Yeah, I don't think that'll be too difficult. It might just mean skipping an extra lunch somewhere. But yeah, I should be able to do that.

MENTOR: Just realize there will be a little give-and-take. As you don't eat out as much, your groceries might increase a little. But the change is probably not going to be as much as what you previously spent. You said you spent about $20 per lunch. It might be $10 more across the groceries. Still a savings, and as you get better at it, then the groceries will probably go down.

You might find the expenses might be a little different in the first couple of weeks as this adjusts itself. That's all right. You've already saved, and then you live within your means. Review and see what else you can do or change. The next time we talk, you'll have $250 saved, and that'll feel good.

MATTHEW: Yeah, that will feel good. I've hardly ever saved anything except for when I was trying to get my car. I ended up getting a loan in the end.

MENTOR: Next time, we will also deal with debt by building a debt plan. In preparation for that, can you get together all the debts you have? This would include a car loan or personal loan, student loans, credit card, Afterpay, Zippay. Get them all together so that we can talk about those next time. All right?

MATTHEW: Yep. No problem.

Fourth Session

Matthew and the mentor talk about reducing debt.

MENTOR: Let's get back to spending and savings. How did it go with your spending spreadsheet? Did you bring your debts along as well? What have you got in debts? Because that's the next stage we need to tackle. You don't want to be paying off debts and investing at the same time. You want to get rid of the things that are costing you and put the money to work for you.

MATTHEW: All right, well, I'm tracking quite well. I could save that money and, through the things I mentioned last week, was able to find the $250 to save. I've got two main debts. I've got my car loan—that's still forty-five hundred dollars. I've paid a little bit of that off, and I pay around about $130 a fortnight. And I've got a credit card, which I don't pay off every month because I don't have enough to do that. I've got a bit of debt on that at the moment, but it's only about five hundred dollars. If I just pay a little bit off each month, then I'll get that down. Oh, and then I've also got Afterpay. I bought some furniture there. I've missed a couple of payments, so that's gone up a little bit as well.

MENTOR: All right, how much is the Afterpay debt?

MATTHEW: It's about six hundred dollars, I think.

MENTOR: Okay, the next step now is to work out which one's the worst debt and which is the best debt, and then go from there.

You've already got 20 percent put aside for savings. Now you're going to take another 10 percent and put it on your debts. Once the debts are gone, that 10 percent goes into your savings, so then you're putting 30 percent in savings. That will really help you build momentum.

MATTHEW: I don't understand.

MENTOR: Right now, you are putting $250 into your savings. Which is what—5 percent of your income per month? If we add up all the loan and debt repayments you make in a month, it is how much?

Matthew nods, though he looks skeptical.

MATTHEW: I have about $355 on repayments at the moment. So about 6.5 percent of my income.

MENTOR: Okay. Give me a minute. I've just put this together. Have a look at this.

Table 3: Matthew's Debt Repayments

Debts			
	Afterpay	Credit Card	Personal Loan
Current Debt	$600	$500	$4500
Monthly Repayments	$150	$75	$130

Normal Method - Remaining Debt			
	Afterpay	Credit Card	Personal Loan
Month 1	$450	$425	$4370
Month 2	$300	$350	$4240
Month 3	$150	$275	$4110
Month 4	Paid Off	$200	$3980

Month 5		$125	$3850
Month 6		$50	$3720
Month 7		Paid Off	$3590
Month 8			$3460
Month 9			$3330
Month 10			$3200
Month 11			$3070
			(Cont...)
Month 32			$340
Month 33			$210
Month 34			$80
Month 35			PAID off

If you keep working on your debts like you are, then in thirty-five months, you should pay off your car and all the other debts.

MATTHEW: That sounds about right, based on what I remember from the car loan document.

MENTOR: What would you say if I could half that time?

MATTHEW: How?

MENTOR: This is a standard debt-reduction process that can quickly reduce debt. It requires a little bit of adherence to a plan but nothing you are not doing already.

MATTHEW: Okay, what is it?

MENTOR: The other good news is, at the end of this process, we want to combine the debt payments and your current savings together and put both of them into your savings. So at the end of this, you'll be putting in nearly 12 percent of your income into savings or about just over $600. However, right now, we want to get those debts cleared because none of those debts are very useful. They got you what you want, but they're not going to help you move forward.

MATTHEW: That sounds nice as well.

MENTOR: Let's work through your debts. From my experience, Afterpay has lots of fees. That's probably the worst one, so we want to get rid of it first. The next worst is probably the credit card because it also has lots of late fees associated with it. Your car loan is going to take the longest, but you've probably got the least number of issues there in terms of late fees and those sorts of things.

Now I want you to put another $100 aside for your debts. I want you to take that money and put it toward Afterpay and get that down. You continue to pay your other debts at their lowest amounts for now.

Once Afterpay debt is gone, we work on the next-lowest debt—which is the credit card. We take all the money we were spending on Afterpay plus the extra $100 plus the minimum amount for the credit card and put all that on the credit card. And keep going. Let me just put this together quickly for you.

Table 4: Debt Management System

Debts			
	Afterpay	Credit Card	Personal Loan
Current Debt	$600	$500	$4500
Monthly Repayments	$150	$75	$130
Additional payments	$100		

Debt Management Method - Remaining Debt				
	Afterpay	Credit Card	Personal Loan	Savings
Month 1	$350	$425	$4370	$500
Month 2	$100	$350	$4240	$750
Month 3	Paid Off	$125	$4110	$1000
Month 4		Paid Off	$3780	$1250
Month 5			$3326	$1500
Month 6			$2872	$1750
Month 7			$2418	$2000
Month 8			$1964	$2250
Month 9			$1510	$2500
Month 10			$1056	$2750
Month 11			$602	$3000
Month 12			$148	$3250
Month 13			PAID off	$3500

Once we have the credit card and Afterpay paid off, the two repayments plus the extra $100 will combine with the repayment for the car loan and start to pay off the car loan. At this stage, that is the whole $454 going on the car loan per month.

Look at this—you will pay out your car loan in thirteen months. Not thirty-five months. That's nearly two years sooner.

MATTHEW: That's amazing. I thought I'd be paying off the car for years, but you're saying in fourteen months, I'll have finished paying it off? Fourteen months and my car is mine?

MENTOR: And you'll also have money in the bank. Remember you are also saving at this time. So you'll also have $3,500 in savings.

MATTHEW: Really?

MENTOR: After fourteen months, you'll start to save $600, so that $3,500 will increase very quickly after that.

MATTHEW: Incredible.

MENTOR: That's what we're going to focus on now. Think about eighteen months from now—you'll be there. If we think about what you will have in terms of savings, you'll have saved up just over four thousand dollars. You've got no debt and four thousand dollars saved.

MATTHEW: I can't believe that. That'll be amazing. I'll have four thousand dollars saved. I'll have no debt. I might already have some sort of investment by then as well because I want to put that money somewhere it's earning more money. And then every month, I'll be putting in quite a lot of money into those savings. That's quite unbelievable.

MENTOR: And that's the power of just taking a few steps at a time. That's the power of patience and endurance. Now, if you didn't do all of those things, you might still be paying off bits and pieces of the credit card. You may have got Afterpay down, or you may still have debt hanging over you. You'd certainly still have the car loan, and you probably wouldn't have any savings. You can see that having a plan and some financial savvy can start you down the right road. Are you willing to give it a try?

MATTHEW: Absolutely.

Your Turn

We covered a lot in this chapter. Sometimes when there is a lot to take in, it can be difficult to know where to start. However, there is probably one area that you can start on straight away to get yourself organized.

Understand your spending habits. I don't use the B-word, as it can scare people. This is not about cutting anything, just awareness. Then you can make decisions based on how strong your Reason is.

Steps to take:

1. Download your bank transactions.
2. Categorize your spending into buckets—groceries, household, health, car, etcetera.
3. Look at the expense totals weekly or monthly or via income period.
4. Look at your income compared to your current expenses.
5. Understand your spending habits. Ask questions like:
   a. How often do you go to the grocery store? Why is that?
   b. What do you spend the most on? Why?
   c. Do you use the things you have subscriptions for (e.g., gym, Netflix, etcetera)?
   d. What repetitive spending do you do? Why?
6. Then decide if these things are still worth the money you spend on them.

"Organization" covers a lot of ground, and I have only scratched the surface. This is where the hard work and consistency pay it forward to your future self. Organizing yourself to work toward a future self whose journey to wealth is ongoing is powerful. In the next chapter, we discuss how important it is also to stay in the moment and have gratitude for where you currently are.

Balancing the now with the future is an important part of wealth creation. You can't live too much in one at the expense of the other. Staying grounded now for a better future is important.

Notes

Notes

Notes

CHAPTER 3
GRATITUDE

Gratitude turns what we have into enough.

—Melody Beattie

In this chapter, we will explore Gratitude and the positive impact it can have on our everyday life and also our future. We will look at how Gratitude will help to reset ourselves and to look for the positive in everything we do. I will give some simple examples of how to do this and what roadblocks you might expect.

We will also see how Matthew (our mentee) starts his journey with Gratitude.

My Story

I'll be honest—gratitude hasn't always been something I've thought about. When I was younger, I was so focused on achieving my financial goals that I spent most of my time looking forward. *What's the next step? How do I get there faster? What do I need to do next?*

It's not that I wasn't grateful for things. I just never stopped to acknowledge them. I had a good job, good health, a supportive family—but I was always chasing the next thing. It was like running on a treadmill. You're moving, but you're not really getting anywhere.

The turning point came when I was working as a well-being officer. I was running surveys and workshops, helping people understand what really contributed to their happiness and well-being. One of the strongest patterns that emerged was this: People who practiced gratitude were consistently happier and more resilient than those who didn't.

At first, I was skeptical. It seemed too simple. Just thinking about what you're grateful for? How could that make a real difference?

With multiple sources indicating the benefits of Gratitude, I decided to try it myself. I started keeping a gratitude journal. Nothing fancy—just a notebook where I'd write down three things I was grateful for each night before bed. On some days, it was big things: my health, my family, my progress toward financial freedom. On other days, it was small things: a good conversation, a sunny afternoon, a problem I'd solved at work.

Within a few weeks, something shifted. I started noticing things I'd previously taken for granted. I felt more content with where I was, even as I continued working toward where I wanted to be. It didn't slow me down—in fact, it gave me more energy and clarity because I wasn't constantly anxious about what I didn't have yet.

Gratitude changed my relationship with wealth creation. Instead of feeling like I was in a constant state of lack—never having enough, never being enough—I started seeing all the progress I'd already made. Every small win became something to celebrate rather than something to rush past on the way to the next goal.

I also noticed it changed how I saw other people. Instead of comparing myself to those who had more, I started appreciating what I had and recognizing that everyone's journey is different.

The comparison game, which is exhausting and pointless, started to lose its grip on me.

That's why gratitude is the *G* in ROGUE. It's not just a nice-to-have. It's essential. Without it, you'll reach your financial goals and still feel empty because you never learned to appreciate what you have along the way.

Why Gratitude Matters

Gratitude isn't just about feeling good—though that's certainly part of it. It's a practical tool that fundamentally changes how you approach wealth creation and life in general.

It shifts your mindset from scarcity to abundance. When you're constantly focused on what you don't have, you operate from a place of scarcity. This leads to anxiety, urgency, and often poor decision-making. You might take unnecessary risks or make impulsive choices because you're desperate to fill that sense of lack.

But when you practice gratitude, you start recognizing what you already have. This doesn't mean you stop striving for more—it means you approach your goals from a place of abundance rather than desperation.

It gives you energy and removes worry. Worrying is exhausting. It drains your mental energy and creativity. When you're constantly worried about what might go wrong or what you don't have, there's less energy left for actually building the life you want.

Gratitude pulls you into the present moment. It reminds you that right now, in this moment, you have things to appreciate. That perspective frees up mental space and energy that was previously consumed by worry.

It helps you celebrate progress. Wealth creation is a long-term journey. If you only celebrate when you reach the final goal, you'll spend years feeling like you're not getting anywhere. That's demotivating and makes it much harder to stay the course.

Gratitude helps you recognize and celebrate the small wins along the way. Paid off a credit card? That's worth acknowledging. Saved your first $1,000? That's progress. These celebrations aren't distractions from your bigger goal—they're fuel for the journey.

It reduces the comparison trap. One of the biggest obstacles to wealth creation is constantly comparing yourself to others. Social media makes this worse—everyone's highlight reel makes it look like they're doing better than you.

Gratitude brings your focus back to your own journey. When you're appreciating what you have and the progress you've made, you're less likely to get derailed by what someone else appears to have.

It makes the destination worth reaching. If you don't practice gratitude along the way, reaching your financial goal won't make you happy. You'll arrive at your destination and immediately start looking for the next thing to chase.

Gratitude ensures that when you reach your goals, you actually enjoy them. You've learned how to appreciate what you have, so you can genuinely savor your achievements rather than rushing past them.

When we talk about gratitude, we're talking about attraction. But if we're blaming, we're pushing away. When we're focusing on gratitude, we're also bringing that into us, making sure that we are looking inward and then making sure that the people around us are understanding what we need to change, and hopefully helping us to make that change.

Gratitude and Wealth Creation

You might wonder what gratitude has to do with building wealth. The connection is deeper than it might seem.

First, gratitude helps you make better financial decisions. When you're operating from scarcity and fear, you're more likely to make impulsive choices—chasing get-rich-quick schemes, taking excessive risks, or spending money to fill an emotional void. Gratitude grounds you. It helps you make decisions from a place of abundance and clarity.

I can give a firsthand account of this when I was on my money journey. I operated from a scarcity mindset. I never thought I had enough or that I would have enough to have wealth. Every decision I made was based on thoughts that I couldn't spend, I didn't have enough to spend the money, or I would be horrible to live with whenever somebody in my family wanted to spend money.

Changing my mindset to one of abundance through Gratitude transformed how I showed up to money conversations. I could see that money was not the only measure of a grateful life and that, in fact, I had made enough and was comfortable now. This allows me to think more rationally about money decisions.

A simple example could be buying a new item of clothing. In the past, I was just looking at the price and making a decision on the price, regardless of the quality or suitability. Once I changed my thought patterns, I started to consider other parts of the purchase decisions such as style, color, reason for wear, country made, quality of fabric, and, of course, price. This made my purchases more enjoyable, and I would often end up with better clothes that lasted longer.

Second, Gratitude helps you stay motivated over the long term. Wealth creation isn't a sprint—it's a marathon. You need something to sustain you through the years of consistent effort. Celebrating your progress through Gratitude provides that fuel. Each time you acknowledge how far you've come, you reinforce your commitment to continue.

Third, Gratitude keeps you from falling into the "enough" trap. Some people work toward wealth, thinking, "Once I have $*X*, I'll be happy." But when they reach that number, they immediately set a new target. The goalpost keeps moving, and happiness is always just out of reach. Gratitude breaks this cycle. It helps you appreciate what you have at each stage, so you can enjoy both the journey and the destination.

Finally, gratitude helps you define what wealth really means to you. Through my work as a well-being officer, I've learned that more money doesn't equal more happiness. The amount of money might vary for each person, but there is a point where more money does not mean more happiness. In fact, it can mean the opposite. What matters is having enough to meet your needs, pursue what's meaningful to you, and help others.

Gratitude helps you recognize when you've reached "enough," so you can focus on living rather than just accumulating. You will recognize this point when money and what it can buy or do for you no longer gives you the most joy. It will be the time when money starts to "buy" you freedom and time. This allows you to be in a place to do what you want.

Gratitude helps in other ways as well.

Invest in "Me" Time

I've spoken to many people and read many books, and one of the biggest things I always hear about is "being busy." A recent survey(s) on time management[11] gave the following statistics on time management:

- Planning Impact: Spending ten to twelve minutes planning the day can save up to two hours of wasted time and effort.
- Work-Life Balance: 36 percent of women and 30 percent of men often feel rushed or pressed for time.
- Wasted Time: Approximately 51 percent to 60 percent of the workday is spent on tasks with little to no value.
- Interruptions: Employees are interrupted roughly sixty times per day, and managers spend about three hours daily dealing with distractions.
- Procrastination: This habit costs the average worker over two hours per day.

We've always got lots of things on. We've got lots of priorities, lots of tasks that need doing. Many times, we're just chasing our own tails. Things don't go as quickly as we think. Things don't happen as easily as we think. And we're constantly trying to complete tasks that we didn't think we'd be doing.

Downtime or time to oneself is not something a lot of people have. Especially if we've got a family, a career, kids to ferry around, and all the usual household chores. We never really have time for ourselves.

11 https://myhours.com/articles/time-management-statistics-2025; https://hubstaff.com/blog/time-management-statistics/; https://www.timewatch.com/blog/time-management-statistics/

One of the things that Gratitude allows us to have is time to spend with ourselves. For some people, this can be very scary. We've built up all this stuff around us to sometimes keep us busy and keep us distracted from ourselves. But gratitude is one way of having a positive impact on our lives and also having some quality me time. Otherwise, you don't really get it.

If you think about it, a lot of times when we're doing things, there's either somebody else there, or there's a distraction—scrolling, reading, gardening. There are other things to think about, but we don't really have positive time just for ourselves. That's what Gratitude is about as well.

We are spending time with ourselves, and we are looking at what we are interested in. We're also writing down the things that made us happy for that particular time. When we do this, we get a little bit more in touch with ourselves.

Now, for some people, this can be quite confronting because often, we don't have time to ourselves or time to think about ourselves. Sometimes we do this on purpose because we don't want to be thinking about the things we could have or the things we don't.

This time is not about just sitting there thinking and then getting depressed about it. You're trying to put a good spin on it and really be in the moment with yourself. You're finding out about yourself—about the things that you like. You might find that after a certain amount of time, you get a better sense of who you are and what gives you joy.

Gratitude is not there to provide some rigid process where you just ask yourself, "Okay, what did I feel grateful for?" It's there to help you understand what makes you happy. What things did you really enjoy? This information, this feedback, can then go back into your reason—to make that more and more aligned with the things you're interested in. It becomes a powerful feedback loop.

Perception

We know that human beings are naturally negative. It's what we are, unfortunately. We have a negative bias, and a lot of that comes from what people call the ancient brain. The ancient brain was designed to keep us safe, to keep us alive. You've probably heard of "fight or flight"—though it's actually three F's now: fight, flight, or freeze.

See the following thoughts on negativity bias:

- Focus on Negativity: Eckhart Tolle[12] observes that the mind can become obsessed with negative thoughts and judgments.
- Fixation on Flaws: C. JoyBell C.[13] highlights how people often fixate on a small, negative detail rather than a "magnificent" whole.
- Survival Mechanism: Psychologists Cacioppo and Berntson[14] explain that focusing on negative outcomes is an evolutionary adaptation for survival.
- Balance Required: Arthur Brooks[15] points out that we need multiple positive emotions to counteract the impact of negative ones.

That was our ancient brain making sure that we had a chance to survive, propagate, and become the dominant force that we are

---

12 https://eckharttolle.com/balancing-negative-emotions/
13 https://www.goodreads.com/author/quotes/4114218.C_JoyBell_C
14 https://psu.pb.unizin.org/psych425/chapter/cacioppo-and-berntsons-1994-evaluative-space-model-esm/; https://www.academia.edu/22999216/Social_Neuroscience
15 https://www.arthurbrooks.com/

now. What it was trying to do was keep us safe. So we have this natural bias toward negativity: "Don't do that because that might be dangerous. Don't do that because that might put you in danger."

Back when the ancient brain was in full effect, we did have a lot of dangers—the environment, wild animals, all sorts of threats. These days, we're in a much safer environment. Yes, I know the news makes it out like everything is awful. You've got to remember, that's such a small percentage of what's going on in the world, and most of what's happening is quite positive. But positive news doesn't sell. It's the negative headlines, the things that shock—they feed into the negative brain. They heighten this idea that we've got to make ourselves safe, that we've got to remove ourselves from danger.

Our perception is often warped to the negative. Initially, it would have been warped to the environment we were in and the animals around us. But now, because a lot of that has gone away, we're shaped by different perceptions. A lot of those perceptions are now based on comparisons—or our own internal comparisons. So we have a negative bias now about ourselves and our abilities. We see the worst in ourselves. We see that we are not good enough. We put ourselves down. This is what that negativity bias is about. We're constantly having these negative thoughts.

What gratitude brings is positive thoughts, positive experiences, positive ideas—things that are going well. Gratitude can be there to stop us comparing or seeing everything in a negative light.

If we go down the road and see that someone has a new car, we naturally think, "Well, why don't I have a new car?" But if you think about Gratitude, you might write something along the lines of, "I was happy that I could go on a trip today." Well, that's all you need, isn't it? All you need is the ability to do those things. It doesn't matter what type of car you have—you can still do those things.

Gratitude is trying to bring you back to yourself and bring your thoughts back to yourself so that you see your current life in a positive way. You're making sure that you're no longer comparing yourself to other things because you're really looking at your life and saying: "What was I grateful for today that made my life easy, fun, safe, secure, content? What was going on for me that made those things good?"

It's not about somebody else's thoughts and feelings about their life or your life. It's about your own thoughts and feelings. Somebody else might say, "Oh, how could you possibly be happy with that?" Well, that's their thought, not yours. You might be very happy with it. When you write it down repeatedly, you reinforce that happiness.

This translates directly into wealth creation. When you see other people doing well, you might think they're doing better than you. You bring that negative thought in.

If we bring it back to the coffee example, you see people constantly bringing their coffees into work. You might think, "I'd love a coffee like that." Sometimes you can have one. But other times, you might think, "Oh, I'm glad I've got a free coffee facility at work. I can have a coffee whenever I want, and I don't have to go out and buy one."

You're saying you don't need to buy something in order to feel good. That Gratitude for the small things can give you the perception that what you were reaching for isn't actually needed. You can stay within what you want, and you don't need to reach for something else that doesn't actually make you happy.

Put another way: Your Gratitude is giving you perception around your wants and needs. You're starting to realize that the wants you have aren't actually doing anything for you in any particular way.

In terms of gratitude, you might say, "OK, I was really happy to save $20 this week because I didn't buy coffees most of the week," instead of saying, "Ah, I had four coffees this week, but they were gone so quickly that they didn't really have any impact on me." But the opposite was true about the $20—"I felt like I saved that, and there was something profoundly powerful about that."

Your perception has changed from what that $20 means to you. This is what we're trying to do with gratitude. We're trying to showcase that perception shift. From a wealth-creation perspective, especially financial-wealth creation, you're using that positivity to reinforce your thoughts around your wealth-creation journey, making sure that you are comfortable and happy with those decisions.

You might find, "Actually, I need my coffee. My coffee makes me really happy in the morning and allows me to have a little bit of social interaction. I'm really happy about that. I might be able to talk with my coworkers, but I don't need to buy my lunch every day because I just go off and eat by myself. I could bring my lunch to work."

You make that distinction because you're feeling that Gratitude, because you're writing those things down. You might have never mentioned lunch, but what you mentioned was, "I love sitting down with people and talking about stuff." The lunch isn't important—it's the connection. So you can bring lunch to work because the lunch itself doesn't matter. But if you say, "I love going out for lunch and chatting with people and having different types of food," and suddenly the food is the important part, that's different.

Hopefully, Gratitude will allow you to understand what's important to you so you can make some of these changes in yourself a little bit easier.

Attraction

There is a quote attributed to Henry Ford: "Whether you think you can or you think you can't, you're right." There have been other quotes of a similar nature, and there are lots of books written about manifesting—*The Secret,*[16] *Think and Grow Rich,*[17] *Manifest.*[18] They're all about this idea of thinking about what you want, focusing on that, and then that will bring it to you.

That's the same thing with what we're doing with Gratitude. Because we have so many negative thoughts, what we're trying to do with Gratitude is change that perception. We're trying to bring in the positive thoughts.

There's been a lot of research done on what we think and what we end up getting and how we perceive it. The brain is a powerful thing. In a lot of the books and research[19] I've read, and in a lot of what I've experienced and taught other people—whatever you think, whatever you constantly think, is what you get.

If you constantly think, "I'm not going to get that promotion," then that's what will happen. Because you do things to make it happen—your brain says, "That's what you want. OK, I'll make that happen." You'll sabotage yourself. You'll say something silly in a meeting.

---

16 *The Secret*—Rhonda Byrne (2006)

17 *Think and Grow Rich*—Napoleon Hill (1937)

18 *Manifest*—Roxie Nafousi (2022)

19 *Unlimited Power*-Anthony Robbins (1986); The Magic of Thinking Big - D.J Schwartz (1959); https://www.psychologytoday.com/au/blog/automatic-you/202507/unlock-your-potential-with-the-power-of-belief;

You won't put in your best effort to get something done. You won't be doing your best. You'll make a project late.

Whereas if you have it at the forefront and you constantly think, "I'm worthy of that promotion," you do everything to get that promotion. You do the extra things. You put in maybe an hour extra every day at work. You double-check things. You go out of your way to be helpful. You're wanting to create that promotion, and you want to give yourself the best chance.

I think a lot of times, people think that manifesting is about just saying, "Okay, I want a promotion," and sitting back. But actually, what happens when you start to think those positive thoughts about wanting a promotion is that your brain will start to help you do the right things to get that promotion.

If you're sitting there and somebody says, "I need some help with this," your brain will say, "Okay, that's the person who's going to have some influence on my promotion. That's my boss. We want to get a promotion. He's going to help us." So you'll volunteer for that. You'll suddenly say, "Yes, I'll help you with that," before you even know what's going on, because your subconscious has already made that decision for you—that this is in line with what you want. That's really what this idea of manifesting is about. It's about defining what you really want, and then you naturally put in the effort to get those things. It isn't about thinking about something and then just sitting back and waiting for it to happen.

With Gratitude, we're trying to do these things as well. We keep writing out the things that we like, that we love, that bring us happiness. That's what Gratitude is about. What are we thankful for? What are we grateful for? We're training our brain that these are the things we're grateful for.

If you write, "I loved that sunrise today" for whatever reason, after you write it a few times, your brain says, "Okay, we feel very comfortable and content when we see the sunrise." Now your brain is going to start to make it easy for you to see a sunrise or sunset, whatever it is. It might make it easier for you to wake up in the morning because it knows that makes you happy.

With the promotion idea, and talking about wealth creation—if you start to say to yourself, "I want to be wealthy because I want to do these things," and during a particular week, you might have said, "I really enjoyed meeting that person and talking about money," or "I really enjoyed that chat with a financial adviser," or "I really enjoyed talking about shares in a real conversation," or "I really enjoyed saving $100 this week"—you get that feeling.

You're replacing negative feelings with positive feelings around money. Your brain then says, "Oh, okay, we enjoyed that part. We've got to do this again because we liked that feeling." So next time somebody talks about money, you think "Let's go talk to this person because last time that was really good." Or "Last time we saved this money, we felt really excited. Let's do that again."

The idea of putting these things into gratitude starts to mean that we will attract those things to us as well. That's what we're trying to do with gratitude. We're trying to put that positivity in there—those things that make us happy—so that we tell our mind: These are the things we want.

When we do some of the wealth-creation work around savings or getting rid of debt, you might put in Gratitude: "I finally removed that debt. I feel so much lighter now and I feel so happy that I've got rid of that debt." And your brain says, "Okay, debt bad. Remove debt good. Okay, I've got that." So you don't want to go into debt.

The next time you're faced with a situation where you might go into debt or have to go into debt to buy something, your brain might create a negative feeling so that you think, "No, we don't want to do this." It might make you say, "I'll save for it instead," or "I'll do something else instead of going into debt." You're starting to build up those resistances about certain things because you've put it into your Gratitude.

How Does All This Help for Wealth Creation?

Wealth creation is about your state of mind. We attract to ourselves what we think. If we think we are poor or undeserving, then we will receive what we think we deserve or maybe not receive what we would like. I have seen it often enough in my work to know this is true, regardless of what I thought about it.

No matter what you do for a living or how you plan to get wealthy, there is always one truth. People like to deal with positive people. We like to be around and help people that help or acknowledge us. Gratitude allows us to get this positive perspective and be a positive influence on those around us. Thinking from a business point of view, would you rather work with a supplier or contractor that is nice to be around or someone that is surly or unresponsive?

The final point of Gratitude is what it does for ourselves. Gratitude can remove the anxiety, frustration, and blindness around our life. It can allow us to appreciate our own little world and thus make us calmer, more content, and more peaceful. This in turn will allow us to experience the world in more joyful ways. If we are more joyful and we are happier, then decisions and discussions (especially about money) can be easier.

How to Practice Gratitude

The good news is that Gratitude is simple to practice. It doesn't require any special tools or a lot of time. Here are some approaches that could work for you.

Keep a Gratitude journal. This is what worked for me, and it's one of the most common and effective methods. Every evening before bed, write down three to five things you're grateful for. They don't all have to be profound. Some days you'll write about major milestones. Other days it might be as simple as "had a good cup of coffee" or "solved a problem at work."

The act of writing forces you to pause and reflect. Over time, you'll start noticing more things to be grateful for throughout your day because your brain is actively looking for them.

To make your Gratitude practice more comprehensive, consider organizing it into categories. For example:

- Personal: things about yourself you appreciate (your health, your efforts, your growth)
- Relational: people in your life and interactions you're grateful for
- Progress: steps you've taken toward your goals
- Simple pleasures: small things that made your day better

This ensures that you're not always focusing on the same things and helps you develop a more well-rounded appreciation for your life.

Practice Gratitude in the moment. You don't have to wait until evening to practice Gratitude. Throughout your day, when something good happens—even something small—pause for a moment and consciously acknowledge it: "I'm grateful for that conversation" or "I appreciate that I have the skills to solve this problem."

These micromoments of Gratitude compound over time and help shift your default mindset toward appreciation.

Share your Gratitude. When you appreciate something someone has done, tell them. Send a message, write a note, or express it in person. This not only strengthens your relationships but also reinforces your own practice of noticing and appreciating the good in your life.

Reflect on challenges. This one might seem counterintuitive, but there's often something to be grateful for, even in difficult situations. Maybe a setback taught you something important. Maybe a challenge revealed your own resilience. You don't have to be grateful for the difficulty itself, but you can appreciate what you learned from it or how you grew through it.

Starting Your Practice

If you're new to Gratitude practice, start simple. Don't try to do everything at once. Pick one approach and commit to it for at least two weeks. The evening Gratitude journal is usually the easiest place to start because it creates a clear routine.

After two weeks, you'll likely notice a shift in how you feel. If it's working for you, keep going. If you want to deepen it, add another category or start practicing Gratitude in the moment throughout your day.

Common Obstacles

Like any practice, Gratitude comes with challenges. Here are some common ones and how to work through them:

- "It feels forced or fake." At first, it might. That's normal. You're building a new mental habit, and like any new habit, it feels awkward before it feels natural. Keep going. Authenticity comes with practice.
- "I had a terrible day—there's nothing to be grateful for." Even on the worst days, there's usually something. Do you have a roof over your head? Running water? A friend who listened? Sometimes having Gratitude on hard days means acknowledging that you got through the day, that you're still here, and that tomorrow is a new day.
- "I keep writing the same things." If you find yourself repeating the same items, challenge yourself to go deeper or broader. Instead of saying, "I'm grateful for my family," try "I'm grateful for the conversation I had with my sister today" or "I'm grateful that my partner made dinner tonight." Getting specific helps you notice new details.
- "I don't have time." This practice takes three to five minutes. If you truly don't have five minutes before bed, your Gratitude practice might need to be acknowledging moments throughout the day instead of writing them down. But honestly, most of us have five minutes. It's about making it a priority.

Remember: You're not just building wealth; you're building a life. Gratitude helps you appreciate that life at every stage of the journey.

Matthew's Journey

First Session

MENTOR: The third letter of ROGUE is for Gratitude. Do you take time out to practice gratitude?

MATTHEW: No. What is it?

MENTOR: Gratitude is a positive psychology tool designed to boost mental and physical health, increase optimism, and reduce stress by shifting focus from negativity to appreciation. Yes, that sounds like a textbook answer, and it is. It's the best one I have come across in my years, and I use it all the time. In a nutshell, it is about documenting the good things in life so we can focus on them. We have so much negativity, so Gratitude journaling is a process to create a bit more of a balance in our thoughts.

I want you to do something between now and next time. I want you to buy a new notepad and start a Gratitude diary. Every day, either in the morning or at night, I want you to write something that you're grateful for on that particular day. I also want you to write one person or thing you're thankful for. You don't have to go and thank them unless you really want to. It might have been somebody at work that picked up the photocopying for you or held the door for you. Whatever it happens to be, just write down somebody you're thankful for.

MATTHEW: Okay. I suppose that shouldn't be too difficult. I've got a notebook I can use.

MENTOR: Please give it a go. This is the part most people struggle with. They think it is weird. What this is going to do is change the way you see the world. We get a lot of negativity coming to us all the time. This is just a way to counterbalance it by getting you thinking about good things. This will start to change your mindset. Most people can find one thing they are grateful for and one person that they are thankful for.

MATTHEW: I can do that, I think. That's a lot to get started with.

MENTOR: The reason Gratitude is important is that it does two things for us in terms of wealth building. It gives us a positive attitude, which will mean we are more open to trying new things and also to learning. As we go through this journey, you will have to do a lot of learning, and there will be new experiences or thoughts that you will have to accept. Gratitude can help in that regard. The second part is removing the comparison trap. As humans, we are very good at comparing without the full picture of another person's life; with Gratitude, we can be thankful for what we have in our life and realize that our life is not so bad. Think "The grass is greener." Gratitude helps us to keep perspective, which can lead to better decisions and higher motivation. It can also help us to understand the things that make us happy.

Second Session

MENTOR: I want to talk about your Gratitude journal. Did you do that?

MATTHEW: I'll be honest. I didn't really get to it. I didn't know where to start.

MENTOR: That can be normal. Probably you were trying to come up with amazing things to be grateful for? Or didn't want to say the same things?

MATTHEW: Yes, that is correct.

MENTOR: That is normal. It really is. However, it is also okay. Sometimes the simplest things are actually the best. For me, watching a sunset can be so inspiring. Do I do it every day? I wish. But when I do, I really try to be in the moment. I do write in my journal so I remember the joy it gives me, and it pushes me to enjoy it as often as I can.

MATTHEW: I didn't think simple would be okay.

MENTOR: There is no "okay." There is only the truth. The truth is what gives you happiness and makes you feel grateful. Did you have trouble doing it regularly?

MATTHEW: Yes. I wasn't sure when to do it. Morning or night? Sometimes I was in a rush and so forgot.

MENTOR: Okay. Let's make it simple. As soon as you put that fork down or that knife down on your plate after dinner, grab your notebook and write out your gratitude items. Whatever they are—no matter how small or how often.

Third Session

MATTHEW: Well, when you said just do it as soon as I put down the fork, it became a lot easier. I kept my book on my dining table, and I started writing something each time I finished dinner. I found it a little bit weird at first, but it just became easier and easier. I found two or three things in each category to be thankful for.

MENTOR: Brilliant. And how did you feel when you were doing that? I mean, I know you said it was awkward at first, but how did it feel as you started doing it more and more?

MATTHEW: I actually really liked it. I was surprised at how I felt about it. It made each day feel good, and it gave me a good feeling for the next day as well. Sometimes when I was at breakfast, I would read the previous day's entry. It was nice to read the things that I was grateful for, and it did actually give me just a little bit more positivity. I felt better when I interacted with colleagues at work. It helped me get along with people better. It changed my thought pattern about people at work. I didn't think it could do that with such a small investment in time.

MENTOR: Well done. There's nothing else that I can say here. Just keep on going. I know you said you've done a couple here and there; now I want you to do it consistently and constantly. Try to increase what you write. Write three or four if you can. And the fact that you started reading them as well is great, because that's how you can build up your internal positivity.

As you start doing this more, you'll realize that this will change how you perceive things. I hope you are also considering yourself and the things you do as well. If not, hopefully you will start to write things that you liked about yourself.

Maybe you'll write, "I was grateful that I was patient with *X* when they were explaining that thing." You build up these things and use them against your limiting beliefs. You use your grateful expression about yourself to showcase you're actually not like that at all. You are a special person. You listen. You're patient. People think you're important.

Those grateful thoughts will start to put doubts into your head about some of your limiting beliefs. And this is how gratefulness can be used as well. It can be used to build evidence to contradict your limiting beliefs. Maybe you think you are always spending. If you have a few entries in your journal about saving or not spending one day, then you can start to break those beliefs.

Continue on, and continue to read it. This is fabulous.

Fourth Session

MENTOR: How did you go with your Gratitude?

Matthew's face lights up.

MATTHEW: Yeah, I've really gotten into it now. I found it quite easy to come up with two things. In the beginning, I didn't realize that I actually had such a good life. I'm really happy with my partner. I think writing it down a lot of times means that some of the fights that we used to have just don't happen anymore because I'm actually coming at it from a different point of view.

I told her what I was doing in terms of Gratitude, and she was quite impressed. She started doing it as well, and now we share our journals once a week and just talk about it. We would have never done something like that. But it's just great. And I see my friends and coworkers at work in a different light. I didn't think this would be anything really amazing, but it's changed my thought patterns. I'm more thankful for what I've got, and I actually stress less.

MENTOR: That's great. You've really embraced it, and you're reaping the benefits, and that's what happens. It doesn't seem like much at first, but it suddenly changes your mindset and how you think about things.

And I mean, that was going to be my next suggestion—to do it with your partner. I'm going to have to come up with something else! But that is exactly what happens. When you want to spread this and you have people on the same page, it just strengthens the bond and strengthens your love for each other. You're thinking of each other in better ways, and you see the good in each other; you're not just always picking out the faults. And sometimes when you have a fight, you can think about your Gratitude for them, and that fight may then become a discussion rather than just an argument. So fantastic.

MATTHEW: Yeah, I'm so pleased. That was the one I was most skeptical about, but I was just going to do it because I thought you would stop talking about it. But now it's the one I'm not stopping. I'll stop maybe some of the other things, but this is just brilliant. It's also made me think a little bit better about myself. I was doing some of the limiting-belief stuff, and I just realized that actually, some of those beliefs are just ridiculous. Especially when I think about some of the good things that I know about myself, I just can't believe that I think negatively about myself at the same time.

MENTOR: Yes, we are complex human beings, and we do like to limit ourselves. I think it's great that you've started to see that, because this is really important. Just keep going down this path and keep on working at it.

Your Turn

This one is easy. Buy an exercise book or start a new document or note. Label it as your Gratitude Journal.

Set aside some time in your day to spend five minutes with your gratitude book or document. Maybe as soon as you get home, or after you brush your teeth, or when you drink your morning coffee. Whenever it seems like you could just take ten minutes to do a small amount of thinking.

Don't overthink it—just write what comes to you to get into a habit.

Notes

Notes

Notes

CHAPTER 4
U IS FOR YOU

Knowing yourself is the beginning of all wisdom.

—Aristotle

What are the things you can do right now to make sure you're ready for the wealth-creation journey? How do you stop yourself from getting in your own way? There are a few simple but powerful places to start. We'll dive into creating the right environment around you, having a clear sense of where you are, understanding your values and attitudes, and building commitment and discipline. These are the parts that make up you, and they all need to line up with your reason if you want to succeed.

My Story

What about me? What did I do?

I can honestly say I didn't know much of this when I started my wealth journey.

Self-sabotage? Why would I do that? Limiting beliefs? What were they, and why would I have any? It took a lot of reading—and a fair amount of trial and error—before I realized that I did have all of those things and more. I knew that if I wanted to succeed, I had to work on myself. Otherwise, I'd keep falling short of where I wanted to be. Or worse, I'd believe that I wanted something I'd been told or read somewhere instead of chasing my own dream. I find from the people I've worked with that human beings are terrible at asking for what they want. They might see something else and think, "That's what I want" because it is safe or it is okay to reach that goal.

For me, three things made the biggest difference: commitment, values, and learning.

Commitment

I had to build discipline around my goal and my reason. One simple example was tracking my expenses. Before spreadsheets and apps made it easy, I did it by hand. And I've done it ever since—for nearly twenty years now. Each time, I look at my history and current spending. What's changed? Am I spending more on something? Why?

At one stage, after starting a new job, I noticed my "Eating Out" costs going up. The first month, I didn't think much of it. The second month, it rose again. Suddenly, I realized that in trying to make new friends and fit in, I was buying lunch every day.

It's the coffee analogy, only bigger. Lunch is about $20 here in Australia. Five days a week, that's $100. Over a year, nearly $5,000.

Table 4: Cost of Lunch by Timeframe

Daily Lunch Cost	Week (5 days)	Month (20 days)	Year (220 days)
$15	$75	$300	$3,300
$20	$100	$400	$4,400
$25	$125	$500	$5,500

That's $4,400 that could go into shares instead of sandwiches.

I made a simple change: Buy lunch on Fridays; bring my own for the rest of the week. Quick, effective, and it stuck.

That's the power of discipline. It's not about deprivation but moderation. If I hadn't kept track of my spending, I could have gone a long time before asking, "Where's my money going?"

Values

I didn't know I had values or even if I did; I didn't know where to find them. I spent some time with other people—experts—discovering my values, asking questions like:

- What is important to me?
- What would I do in certain situations?
- How would I react in certain events?
- How would I choose one thing or another?

Through these and other questions, I started to understand my value order. I understood what was important to me and how the values I had impacted the decisions I made and how I made them.

This meant that I wasn't fighting myself when I did things or made decisions because I knew my number value. I talked about congruence earlier in the book. This was the same here. If you are making decisions not in line with your values, then you will start to self-sabotage yourself because you want to be congruent with yourself.

I noticed in life that my values have changed as major life events happened. Your values when you are a single individual differ from when you are in a family. You should always reevaluate your values when life events happen.

Learning

I've been fairly lucky in my life, as I have had a thirst for knowledge from a very young age. I always wanted to know things, and I had a very good memory for facts. This was around self-discovery as well as learning about investment ideas.

That's how I first heard about crypto, back around 2017. I wasn't ready then, but I collected bits of information. Years later, I decided to dive in. I listened to the wrong voice, went in too fast, and lost around $150,000 to a scam. Painful, yes—but also a powerful lesson.

I had the curiosity but not the diligence.

I believed what someone else told me and didn't do the learning myself. I didn't understand enough, and I didn't want to miss out. (FOMO, anyone?) I rushed in and hoped it would be okay in the end.

This was not my usual practice. Normally, I would research to get more than a good understanding and then test the waters with small amounts of money and time before deciding whether it fits with me. Thankfully, not all my investment decisions were so painful.

I made quite a few property investments across three countries that helped me slowly build wealth over time. I invested time into understanding property and learned a lot about it before I started. I attended seminars and read a lot of books and discovered the reasons for property investment and the things I should know and do.

Due to the long-term nature of property investing, I was able to iron out any mistakes made—mistakes that might have cost me more, such as picking the wrong property, picking the wrong suburb, picking the wrong type of property, or picking the wrong property agent or tenant. The list is quite long.

One of the biggest lessons or learnings was about my own money journey.[20] When I first started on my wealth journey, I didn't know there was something called a money journey. The following were statements that I heard and internalized:

- Money doesn't grow on trees.
- Cents will become dollars.
- Work smarter, not harder.
- Money is just a tool.

There were others, but these stuck with me the most, and I have repeated them to people as well, so they must have been deeply imprinted. But what did it mean?

For me these expressions meant:

- I needed to work hard for my money; it just wasn't going to come to me.
- All my little savings would become big savings.
- Hard work is important, but I must also look to leverage my own capabilities with others.
- Money is not happiness, but it can help to create (buy) the things I want or need.

I understood what money was for me in the context of my journey.

---

20 A money journey is a personal, lifelong process of managing, growing, and aligning financial resources with one's life goals, values, and purpose. It bridges financial planning (budgeting, investing) with emotional, psychological, and behavioral shifts, moving from a scarcity mindset toward abundance and financial freedom.

Understanding Your Money Journey

Over the next few sections, I'm going to delve into a lot of concepts to help us understand ourselves and our relationship with money. You are going to have a look at your personality. We are going to create our value order, and we are going to start on overcoming our own negativity bias. We are also going to look at the things that create our negativity bias.

Money Thoughts

What's your relationship with money? What stories do you tell yourself? What things do you believe?

"I never have enough."

"Money slips through my fingers."

"I'm just not good with money."

Say those things often enough, and they become self-fulfilling. You start living them out without even realizing it. The first step to understanding your money journey and the thoughts that have imprinted on your brain about money is to become aware of what you're saying to and about yourself, then change the script.

Billy Graham once said, "If a person gets his attitude toward money straight, it will help straighten out almost every other area of his life." What you tell yourself might be exactly what you get.

This is important. We have already touched on attraction in the chapter concerning Gratitude, and this feeds directly into those thoughts. What you think about money and how you perceive it play a part in how you will perceive yourself when you have money.

If you think that "all rich people are liars" or "all rich people are only out for themselves," then you will not want to become a rich person. You will do everything to not be a rich person for the simple fact that you don't see yourself as a liar or selfish. The same is true for any other negative thoughts.

Understanding Your Personality Type

One tool many people overlook, but which I found incredibly valuable, is understanding your personality type. I know some people scoff at personality tests—they think it's just putting people in boxes or limiting who they can be. But personality tests aren't about pigeonholing you. They're about giving you insight into how you naturally operate—your strengths, your weaknesses, and how you're likely to react in different situations. When you understand yourself better, you can work with your natural tendencies rather than fighting against them.

The framework I want to focus on here is the one from the book *Surrounded by Idiots.*[21] This model uses four colors—Red, Green, Blue, and Yellow—to represent different personality types.

It's important to remember that nobody is purely one type. Most of us are a blend, with perhaps one or two dominant traits. The goal isn't to fit yourself neatly into a category—it's to recognize patterns in how you think and behave so you can leverage your strengths and work on your weaknesses. Understanding who you are helps you to stay on course with your Reason but also understand how you will react in times of pressure, frustration, and pain. All of these will appear as you journey on your road to wealth.

---

21 *Surrounded by Idiots*—Thomas Erikson (2014).

The Red Personality

Red personalities are natural leaders. They're the CEOs, the decision-makers, the people who get things done. If you're a Red, you probably make decisions quickly, you're very direct, and you have no patience for fluff or unnecessary chitchat. You like to direct the path forward, and you're comfortable taking charge. Reds tend to follow the 80/20 rule instinctively—they focus on the 20 percent of actions that will produce 80 percent of the results.

But every strength has its shadow side. The Red personality's directness can come across as brusque or even rude. They're often already thinking about the next thing while someone else is still talking. They might not be as concerned with people's feelings, which can create barriers in relationships. And here's the classic one: Reds tend to think everyone else is an idiot.

If you're building wealth, this matters. You're going to need help—an accountant, a financial adviser, a broker, maybe a property conveyancer or lawyer. These are people with expertise, and they expect to be listened to. If you walk into meetings thinking you know everything already, you're not going to get the value you're paying for.

So if you recognize yourself as a Red, here's a tip: When you're meeting with experts, put your Red tendencies in a bottle for a moment. Go in with an open mind. Listen. Ask questions. You can still be decisive and action oriented, but make sure you're gathering all the information first. People who have knowledge like to share it—and you'll benefit from letting them.

The Green Personality

Green personalities are easygoing, steady, and reliable. They value harmony and stability. If you're a Green, you're probably someone people can count on. You're patient and supportive, and you don't like rocking the boat.

The strengths of a Green are their consistency and loyalty. They build strong, lasting relationships, and they're excellent team players. They create calm, stable environments.

But here's the challenge: Greens don't like change. And wealth creation—especially in the beginning—involves a lot of change. You'll need to adjust your spending habits, try new investment strategies, and step outside your comfort zone. If you're a Green, this is going to feel uncomfortable. Change might feel threatening, even when you know intellectually that it's good for you.

So if you're a Green, be aware of this tendency. Recognize when your resistance to change is protecting you from genuine risk—and when it's just holding you back from growth. Build change into your plan gradually. Small steps are your friends. You don't have to transform overnight. Just keep moving forward, even if it's slower than others might move.

The Blue Personality

Blue personalities are the analysts. If you're a Blue, you love detail, precision, and accuracy. You want all the information before you make a decision. You're thorough and methodical, and you don't like making mistakes.

This is a tremendous strength when it comes to wealth creation. Blues do their research. They understand the fine print. They don't rush into things without due diligence. These qualities can save you from costly mistakes.

But Blues can also get stuck in analysis paralysis. You want more detail, then more detail, then even more detail. At some point, you have to make a decision and take action. If you're waiting for all the information, you'll never move forward—because perfect information doesn't exist.

If you're a Blue, recognize when you have enough information to make a sound decision. Set deadlines for yourself. "I'll research this for two weeks, and then I'll decide." And remember: Not every expert or adviser will give you every single detail you're craving. Sometimes you need to trust their expertise without knowing every microelement of how they reached their conclusion.

The Yellow Personality

Yellow personalities are the enthusiasts. They're optimistic, social, creative, and spontaneous. If you're a Yellow, you're probably the life of the party. You build relationships easily, you're inspiring to be around, and you bring energy and ideas to everything you do.

Yellows are great at networking, which can be incredibly valuable for wealth creation. You naturally build the relationships you need with advisers, mentors, and opportunities. Your optimism helps you bounce back from setbacks.

But Yellows can struggle with follow-through and discipline. You're excited about new ideas, but you might jump from one thing to the next without finishing what you started. Details bore you. Structure feels restrictive. And your optimism, while generally a strength, can sometimes blind you to real risks.

If you're a Yellow, you'll benefit from creating systems and structures that keep you on track without killing your enthusiasm. Automate your savings. Set up regular reviews with an accountability partner. And be honest with yourself about when your optimism needs to be tempered with a realistic assessment of risk.

My Personality

I have strong parts Red and Blue, with a little Green. I research things and make quick decisions. These three components help me in most of my investment decisions, as they allow me to be decisive about what information I need, look to the numbers to make decisions, and evaluate things quickly.

These combinations can be bad when I overresearch or when I am short with people when they don't think as quickly as I can or can't see the lines of logic into the future. I can be rude or abrasive and think that my time is the most important thing in the world.

I've had to do a lot of work on myself to keep the strengths but control my weaknesses. My strengths were helping me on my way to my Reason; however my weaknesses were pushing people away. I also found out that I wasn't always the smartest person in the world (shock and horror) and that a lot of people have good information and experience to impart.

Using Your Personality Insights

The point of understanding your personality type isn't to use it as an excuse. "That's just how I am" isn't a free pass to avoid working on your weaknesses. Instead, it's about self-awareness.

When you know your natural tendencies, you can:

1. Leverage your strengths. If you're a Red, use your decisiveness. If you're a Blue, use your analytical skills. Play to what you naturally do well.
2. Compensate for your weaknesses. If you're a Green who struggles with change, acknowledge that and build in support. If you're a Yellow who struggles with follow-through, create accountability systems.
3. Communicate better with others. If you're a Red, stop, relax, and talk slowly. If you're a Blue, don't bore them with all the details.
4. Recognize patterns in your behavior. When you find yourself reacting in a certain way—impatient with details, resistant to change, stuck in analysis—you can catch it and ask, "Is this my personality type speaking, or is this a genuine concern?"

Everyone is unique. These personality types are guides, not boxes. You might be primarily one color with strong elements of another. The value is in the insight, not in the label.

I'd encourage you to explore these frameworks. Read *Surrounded by Idiots* if you haven't already. Take a Myers-Briggs personality test. Think about how your personality shaped or is shaping your values. The more you understand about yourself, the better equipped you'll be to build wealth in a way that works with who you are, not against it.

In the next sections, we will continue our self-discovery journey beyond your personality into the realm of values and achievements.

Some Self-Discovery Exercises

The unexamined life is not worth living.

—Socrates

As mentioned in the introduction to this chapter, values are something everyone has, but sometimes they are not obvious until we explore ourselves. This is especially true when it comes to money and our attitude or values around it.

When I did this work on myself, it was amazing what I discovered.

We grow up surrounded by messages about money—some useful, some toxic. A common one is that "money is evil" or that "rich people are selfish." We hear it in movies, TV shows, even crime stories—money as the root of greed or betrayal. Money or love are the most likely reasons in a crime show for someone to do harm to another.

Imagine wanting money but also believing deep down that having it makes you a bad person. That's a conflict—and it sits quietly in the background, sabotaging your success.

You have to reconcile those two ideas. Having money doesn't make you Scrooge. It gives you freedom, choices, and opportunities—to be generous, to support causes, to create things. Wealth amplifies who you already are.

Here are practical, repeatable exercises I use to get clearer about who I am and what I want.

Sticky-Note Values

Grab a stack of sticky notes and follow this process:

1. Write one value per note: family, health, learning, generosity, wealth, travel, work, service, honesty, ambition, security, excellence, trust, integrity—anything that matters to you.
2. Stick the first note on a wall, then pick the next one and decide which of the two matters more.
3. Whichever is secondary, put it below the higher value.
4. Keep comparing and stacking until the notes are ranked.
5. Leave the list on the wall for a week. Come back and see whether the order still feels right. Refine it.
6. Repeat in a month.

This simple sorting exercise forces clarity. When a tough choice arrives ("Do I go to the gym or have drinks with friends?"), you'll already know which value wins because you chose it consciously.

Ask yourself questions are you go along and be honest—you don't have to tell anyone your values, but it will certainly help you:

- Make comparison questions (like above) and see what comes out on first impression.
- What does your gut say?
- What does your heart say?
- Put things in the context of "If this was my last dollar, would I spend it on *X* or *Y*?"
- Is this a real answer, or am I being socially aware of what I should say?

My Values

I did this exercise early on in life, and I have repeated it on many occasions to understand whether things have changed after major life events. Values are beliefs that help guide your behaviours, decisions, and life direction. Knowing your own will help you understand why you might have made certain decisions or not.

For myself, I initially (just after finishing university) had the following top five values:

1. Learning
2. Security
3. Friends / Fun
4. Health
5. Career

Later in life, these changed based on events and age. My values are more like this now:

1. Family
2. Security
3. Health
4. Travel
5. Safety

For some people, safety and security might be the same thing. For me, safety was about a physical need, and security was about a financial need.

In terms of wealth creation, knowing your values can help with making sure your Reason includes your core values, making it easier for you to stay on track.

Next we will look at your achievements. You will notice how many of the ones you are most proud of align with your values.

Write Your Achievements

Most of us have a bias toward negative thinking. Small setbacks cause us to spiral and drown out the wins. One antidote is to write out your accomplishments—big and small. Things like:

- Got my driver's licence.
- Landed my first job.
- Finished a course.
- Helped a friend through a crisis.
- Raised a kid.
- Finished a project (be specific).

Make a list. It builds a muscle of self-worth. You'll be surprised how long that list becomes and how it steadies you when impostor syndrome creeps in.

The Inner Blockers

Before we move on from U (You), there are three big personal blockers that most of us run into sooner or later: limiting beliefs, fear (headlined by impostor syndrome), and gratification. Each one can quietly sabotage your progress if you don't face it head-on. The good news? You can work through every one of them. Let's break them down.

Limiting Beliefs

We've already talked about belief, but we also need to face its darker twin—limiting beliefs. These are really just fears that have found a home inside you. Thoughts like "I'm not good enough," "I don't deserve money," "No one would want to do business with me," or "I'm not the kind of person who succeeds."

Sound familiar? We've all got a few of these running in the background. They don't make us special or broken—just human. What does make a difference is what we do with them. The people who rise above these beliefs don't give them airtime. They don't let them take up space in their heads.

When it comes to your own limiting beliefs, the first step is to drag them into the light. Write them down. Every time one surfaces—"Why am I even doing this?" or "No one will care"—get it on paper. Then answer it. Challenge it.

"Why am I doing this?" Because I want to be financially free. Because I want choices. Because I'm capable.

Every time you counter that inner critic, its voice gets smaller. Over time, you'll barely hear it. I've had my fair share of limiting beliefs—"not good enough" has been a big one for me, and honestly, it still pops up. The trick is to meet it head-on with evidence: the skills you've learned, the wins you've had, the effort you've shown. Your list of what you can do will always outshine what you can't.

Fear

Fear is the number one thing that stops us doing what we want to do. And it's never just one fear—it's a whole family of them. Fear of failure, fear of looking foolish, fear of missing out, fear of rejection, fear of losing money. The list goes on.

But the cure for fear is simple, even if it's not easy: action. When you take action, fear loses its grip. The moment you start doing, the overthinking stops.

I used to hate networking events—walking into a room full of strangers made my skin crawl. But once I started attending investment and property seminars, I had to face it. My "cures" were a few simple actions: Smile, walk up, introduce myself, and ask questions. "Hi, I'm Stefan, good to meet you." Then I'd ask, "What do you do?" or "What did you think of tonight's talk?" That tiny bit of structure—and a smile—took all the fear out of it.

The same goes for fear of failure. Nobody wants to fail, but it's inevitable if you're doing anything worthwhile. The trick is to reframe it. Don't see it as failure—see it as feedback. Every mistake teaches you something that no book or mentor ever could. Just make sure you take the time to learn from it so that you don't repeat it.

And remember: You'll never have total control over everything. Not your investments, not your job, not your kids, not even your dog. The only thing you can control is how you respond. When you take full responsibility for yourself, fear loses its power.

Impostor Syndrome: Rules Beat Rumination

Impostor syndrome is a cheeky thief: It steals confidence and leaves you second-guessing. Impostor syndrome is a persistent, internalized fear of being exposed as a "fraud" or "phony," despite documented success, competence, and evidence of ability. Individuals with this psychological phenomenon often feel undeserving of their achievements, attributing success to luck or external factors rather than their own skills. I still feel it sometimes.

My remedy has been to write self-help rules for myself. Rules reduce friction and remove the need to endlessly debate. They help in three ways:

1. Decision rules (e.g., "I will review any potential share investment against these five criteria").
2. Process rules (e.g., "I check expenditures monthly and adjust").
3. Guardrail rules (e.g., "If a deal seems too good to be true, pause for seventy-two hours and seek independent advice").

Rules don't make you rigid; they free willpower and cut the noise that feeds self-doubt. Self-doubt is not something you can entertain when you are making decisions about money and your financial future.

When coming up to a big money decision and you are worried, ask yourself (and other questions like them):

- Have you done the research?
- Are you being driven by fear or logic?
- Are you thinking with scarcity or abundance?
- Is this the real thing or an impostor thinking?

These questions will (hopefully) bring you back to yourself and allow you to make more rational decisions—not ones based on fear emotions. Fear is good up to a point, but you don't want it to make the decisions.

Gratification

Now, let's talk about gratification.

This can be where a lot of people come unstuck. There is a difference between a reward and gratification. A reward is planned and received for completing some task. Gratification is about pleasing yourself with a gift just because you think you should have one. You need to distinguish between them in your mind. One will incentivize you to keep going on your wealth journey; one will delay you reaching your goal.

If every time you see money in your account and you start planning your next purchase, you'll never build wealth. You'll just build clutter.

That's why your reason—your big "why"—is so important. When you're about to spend, ask yourself: "Does this move me closer to my Reason?"

Sometimes the answer will be yes.

There are things that will bring you closer to your wealth-creation goal; however, you should use these as rewards. Such as investing in a course, attending a workshop, learning something new—all of that feeds your long-term vision.

But buying something just because it's on sale? That's not building wealth. That's building regret.

Think about the next time you see end-of-the-year sales or Black Friday sales. You may see an item on sale that is just a really good price (60 percent off) but not something that you really need, but it would look nice, or you'd like to use it. You think it's on sale, so it is a bargain: "I'm saving money on it." You buy it, maybe use it once or twice, and then it goes in the back of the cupboard, likely never to be used again. After a few years, you find it and then just get rid of it since you don't need it anymore.

Would you have been better by stopping the purchase and asking, "Do I need this?" or "Is this getting me closer to my goals?" or "Is this something I can't do without?" or "Should I think about it overnight and then see if I still need it tomorrow?"

Depending on what your answers are, you might have to explore what the reason is behind this. If you still need it to fulfill some internal need, then what are you missing? What need are you trying to fill? This will be important to figure out so you don't keep sabotaging yourself. This might be work you need to do with a counselor or other health professional.

Willpower

Then there's willpower. Most of us think it's unlimited—it's not. Research in books like *Deep Work*[22] and *The One Thing*[23] shows that willpower depletes over the day. That's why diets fail at night and bad habits creep in after work.

Knowing this can help you avoid some traps or pitfalls toward the end of the day when we are at our weakest.

I used to buy hot chips on my way home from work in the UK. It was my little treat. But over time, it became a habit—a costly one in both health and money. The fix? I changed my route to the station so I wouldn't pass the chip shop. Simple, but powerful. I didn't have to test my willpower when it was depleted. I was always going to fail, and then the cycle of guilt took over as well.

---

22 *Deep Work*—Cal Newport (2016)
23 *The One Thing*—Gary Keller and Jay Papasan (2013)

We often punish ourselves when we slip up on the road to our goals. We berate and curse ourselves that we should be better. However, sometimes it is not about berating ourselves; it is also about knowing our psychology: how our mind works. This is what understanding yourself is all about. Knowing that your willpower depletes rather than being unlimited means you can do other things at other times or in other ways to avoid falling into bad habits.

You don't conquer bad habits through brute force—you outsmart them.

Conserve your willpower. Use it early in the day on what matters most. Save it for the things that move you closer to your reason.

Moving Forward

By now, you've done a lot of heavy lifting. You've found your Reason—the vision that pulls you forward. You've learned to get Organized and take action. You've built Gratitude into your daily mindset, and you've faced You—your tendencies, weaknesses, and blocks.

That's a huge amount of inner work, and for most people, it's enough to start seeing results. But wealth creation—real, lasting financial freedom—doesn't come from what you do once. It comes from what you keep doing, even when progress slows, motivation dips, or the results take longer than you'd hoped.

That's where the final piece of the ROGUE mindset comes in: Endurance. Endurance isn't just about grinding through—it's about staying consistent, patient, and purposeful over time. It's about showing up, again and again, long after the excitement has worn off.

If you've done the first four steps, you've already built the foundation for it. Now, let's talk about how to keep going when the initial spark fades—and why Endurance is the real secret to becoming financially free.

Matthew's Journey

Matthew's journey around money and self-discovery is very important; however, it will take many sessions to work through this.

First Session

MENTOR: Although U is the second last letter of ROGUE, it is one of the most important parts. U is about you and the work you need to do on yourself in order to be ready to accept your wealth and everything that comes with that. This will also take the longest to do. You never stop growing or learning. This will also be the most confrontational. This part is getting to know you. Maybe you already know yourself; then great, but most people I work with still have a lot to learn about themselves.

The first thing we are going to tackle is your money journey. This comes in a few ways—our habits and our thoughts. You are probably not aware of what you do or think in terms of money. Most people don't; they do them unconsciously. We want to bring them to consciousness. Become aware of them and know them.

As you do all your normal things this next month, I want you to write down what you think some of your money habits are. You'll probably see these as you go along, and you'll start to notice them. Can you think of any so far?

MATTHEW: I don't think so.

MENTOR: Let me give you some examples of the things I mean:

- You buy a coffee every day at work.
- You go to the gym.
- You buy lots of groceries but normally don't use them all.

- You impulsively buy things online.
- You can't leave a bookshop without buying a new book.
- You socialize in some form every day or every Friday.
- You struggle to pay your bills when they come in.
- Money never stays in your account; it is spent.

MATTHEW: I can do that.

MENTOR: I'm not judging. Everyone has these habits. The next thing I want you to write down next to these habits is the thought or feeling you had when you did it. These can be simple, like:

- I need a break.
- I've worked hard; I should be able to play hard.
- I deserve a little treat.
- I've had a tough day; I need some relaxation.
- I want to be part of the group or everyone else is doing it.
- I just need to talk to someone instead of looking at a computer.
- I hate not having enough money.
- Money is there to be spent.

MATTHEW: Okay.

MENTOR: This might seem strange or difficult to feel the "feeling" in the moment. Don't force it. If you don't know, then just leave it blank.

Write down anything you can. If not the "feeling," then maybe how you were feeling—tired, bored, excited.

MATTHEW: I can do that.

MATTHEW: How is this going to help me make money? Or build wealth?

MENTOR: Good question. Let's look at an example. Next time we are going to look at getting savings together, so let's start with that. How would you do it?

MATTHEW: I'd maybe leave $50 in my account and not spend it. Then do the same the next week.

MENTOR: All right. I would say that probably hasn't worked in the past; otherwise, you would already have savings. What happens to those savings?

MATTHEW: I normally have a night out, or some big bill comes that I need to pay for.

MENTOR: That's right. Then the money we save is gone, and we have to start again. Normally it takes a while because the guilt needs to be overcome about spending the "savings" money.

So we need to start before that and understand why you do things. We also need to know your mindset to see what your thoughts are on money. There is a lot of research that suggests our unconscious mind predicts what we will get from life. To put that very plainly, if we think we are worthy of money, then we will keep it; if we think we are not, then we spend it. That might sound very simple, but it gets to the heart of the research.

In terms of the savings, we need to understand why you keep spending the money and not keeping it. Then we need to figure out where the money might come from. Then we need a system to keep the money in your account. Once we do all that, then you might be able to save some money.

MATTHEW: That makes sense, I suppose.

MENTOR: I have an exercise for you to think about before the next session. If, at the next session, I were to give you $1,000, what would you do with it? And don't tell me what you think I want to hear. Honestly tell me what you would do with it. I'm not judging. It is just a question.

MATTHEW: Okay, I can do that.

Second Session

MENTOR: Let's start with the money journey. Remember the $1,000 question. What would you do?

MATTHEW: Yeah, so I had two thoughts. First, I've been wanting to go to Melbourne for ages, so I was thinking about going down there and seeing a mate and taking my partner on a little holiday. And second, it's funny now I think about it, there's this punching bag that I've been wanting to buy. I thought I'd get that because that would be just below $1,000, and then the rest, I'd just leave in my account.

MENTOR: All right. Well, that's great. I'm glad you did that.

MATTHEW: Is that good or bad?

MENTOR: It is neither. It just is, and it tells us something about you.

MATTHEW: What?

MENTOR: Listening to yourself, what does it tell you?

MATTHEW: That I thought about spending first and then maybe saving is not in line with what I want.

MENTOR: Good. What else?

MATTHEW: I'm not sure. Maybe I like treating myself. I got a thrill thinking about the things I could buy.

MENTOR: Those are good insights. This is a journey of self-discovery. It will get easier as we go further together. What about habits and thoughts? Did you go through that?

MATTHEW: Yes, I got some things written down. To summarize, I did realize that I often call myself stupid, or it's no wonder that I'm just a data analyst and those sorts of things. I have some beliefs that I'm not very good at my job.

MENTOR: Okay, this is good but not quite what we discussed. We probably need to work on that at some time as well. I appreciate you telling me those things. It links up with your comments above. What about your habits and thoughts around them?

MATTHEW: I did realize I bought my lunch out a lot. The feeling that goes with that is relaxation and relief. I drive past the gym and don't go in, even though I have the membership; there is guilt there. I feel I never have money, there's guilt, and I feel stupid. I have a big bill coming, and I'm stressed about it. I bought a new yoga mat the other day, and I felt better and excited. I didn't need it and haven't used it yet.

MENTOR: Okay, those are good. I mean, it is great you are being honest and can identify your emotions. I have a question. We were talking about savings earlier. This requires some more money, obviously. How would you look to get this extra money?

MATTHEW: I'd probably try to get a raise at work. That seems the easiest way. I don't want to start a side hustle. I wouldn't know what to do.

MENTOR: Okay, that's fine. Consider this scenario. You've been asked by your boss to ring up a client that you did some work for because they were not quite happy with what you'd done. He wasn't sure what the issue was, and he just wanted to get it clarified. What would be your thoughts there?

MATTHEW: I don't talk to clients at all. I'd be bloody nervous. I wouldn't want to know what they said. Oh, I don't know what I'd do there. It'd take me a while to pick up the phone, I think. I hate it when people don't like my work. I always try to do my best, but when somebody gives me criticism, I clam up and I don't talk and I can't handle it. And I just think, "What an idiot. Why didn't I get this right the first time?" It would take me ages to get on the phone to them. I don't like talking on the phone. I like talking face-to-face.

MENTOR: All right, could you go see them?

MATTHEW: Oh, that would be even worse. That would be even worse to go see them. Then they could maybe yell at me. Down the phone, at least I can hold the speaker away. I'd be worried the whole time.

MENTOR: If you were to get a promotion, this would likely be most of your day. Extra money means more responsibility. In white-collar workers, it means working with people, whether that is clients or workers. That's how the world works.

MATTHEW: I don't want to work with people.

MENTOR: So a promotion might not be the way to get extra money.

MATTHEW: Maybe not.

MENTOR: This might seem random, but you would have sabotaged yourself from getting that promotion because of what you just said you don't want to do. You want to stay where you are. At least for now. This is okay. However, if you are thinking one thing and feeling another, your feelings will always win.

Fears of missing out or fears of feeling foolish are strong drivers of action or inaction.

There is also the other side of the coin. Imagine you've gone into a meeting with your boss and he says, "I didn't want to do this in front of everybody, but I wanted to tell you that I got a call from a client the other day, and they couldn't stop raving about the work that you'd done for them. They were really happy. I'm impressed. This is the type of work that we want people to see, and I know you've worked so hard on this."

The boss is smiling at you, waiting for you to say something. What do you do?

MATTHEW: All right. I wouldn't believe him, really. Everybody else works pretty hard, and I'm just doing my job, so I'm not anything special. I'm just getting on with what I need to do. It's nice to hear, but it's not going to really do much for me, I think. Yeah, maybe James, who does some of the bigger dashboard stuff, he's the one that's really knocking it out of the park. He's the one that should get this praise. I'd probably just sit there, say thanks, and then if that was it, I'd probably just go.

MENTOR: That's good to know. When somebody praises you, you don't think it really means much? Is that what you're saying?

MATTHEW: Well, everybody else does good work. Most do harder stuff than me. Why should I be singled out?

MENTOR: All right. There's some really good questions there and some really good answers. Thank you for being honest. Those two responses—fear of feeling foolish and then not wanting to be "singled out"—are standard responses and feelings. However, they hold you back.

If an aunt left you some money, a decent amount of money, what would you think?

MATTHEW: Great. I'd probably spend it on a house. Or new car.

MENTOR: Which is more likely?

MATTHEW: The car.

MENTOR: Again, showing you don't think you are worthy. You are "throwing" the money away.

MATTHEW: A car is worth something.

MENTOR: But it is not an asset. Assets put money into your pocket. Liabilities take money out of your pocket. Did you get any other thoughts about money?

MATTHEW: I did a little bit. My parents were working class; my dad was a truck driver, and my mom was a nurse. They both had good work ethics. I think the one I heard the most was from my father who used to say all the time, "Money doesn't grow on trees." I heard that heaps and I also heard a lot of times, "You'll be all right; we don't need that." A lot of times, I did without. I wasn't happy about it, but there was no other choice. I saw some other kids who'd get stuff and sometimes be envious of them. But I dealt with those feelings.

MENTOR: All right. Well, I think this has been really great, and there's a lot of things that I want you to continue to do here. Last thing. Have you ever taken a personality test before?

MATTHEW: No, I haven't.

MENTOR: Okay, I'll send you an extract from a book. Read it and see which color links up to your personality. You can have two or three colors. Keep going on the money journey—writing things down as they come to you. Write down the positives and the negatives. They are about building awareness in your attitudes to money.

Third Session

MENTOR: We have a few things to cover under U today. I asked about a personality test. I asked to do more work on awareness of money thoughts. I also wanted you to reflect on your thoughts of yourself. How did all that go?

MATTHEW: Yeah, well, I struggled with that quite a bit actually. I just kept thinking, "Who am I to do something like this?" There are so many other better people in the world that can do this. There are people out there already doing this. I'm like, "Who am I to do this?" It really got me thinking that this is too big. I did write those thoughts down, like you asked.

Another one that came out when I started thinking about money: Why do I think that I deserve such wealth and not somebody else? Why am I so special to do this? I also thought, "What happens if I don't get this done? I'd just feel such a fool. I feel I can't even talk to anybody about this."

MENTOR: I understand. This might sound harsh. However, those thoughts are natural and normal.

MATTHEW: Doesn't make it any better.

MENTOR: I know. This is fear coming out. Fear keeps us from change. Fear keeps us comfortable. Fear is the animal brain trying to keep us safe.

MATTHEW: Animal brain?

MENTOR: I don't want to go too deeply. There are many parts of the brain. One is the animal brain, which has been trying to keep us, both individually and as a species, safe for thousands of years. However, times have changed, and we are not in so much physical danger, but our brain is still trying to keep us safe.

MATTHEW: Sure.

MENTOR: Now, just because we've identified these fears doesn't mean that they're going to go away. But identification and awareness of them is the first step. What you've done here is fantastic. Do you understand where these fears and beliefs came from?

MATTHEW: No, not really. I didn't think about it. It made me feel quite negative, and I didn't want to think about it. My motivation went really flat.

MENTOR: Yeah, I can hear it in your voice now. Hearing you, I see you're very flat and your energy is really low. I want you to realize that's what your limiting beliefs do. This is what these thoughts are—they are called limiting beliefs, and they are what they say. They are beliefs that limit our progression. They bring you down. They put your energy low so you don't want to start anything, and you feel like you can't get anywhere. This is where we want to make those changes and do those in a slow, steady way so that you can feel like you're moving forward and that these things don't hold you back.

We will be working through this over time. Time is what you have—remember Endurance. It doesn't have to be all done today. "Rome wasn't built in a day."

You learned so much about yourself. Let's summarize those fears or limiting beliefs:

- Fear of being foolish.
- Fear not being part of the crowd.
- Why me?
- Other people are more important than me.
- It all seems so big.

We will add to this as we go.

I want you to imagine this week somebody comes up to you and you say to them, "I'm worth a million dollars." And they say, "Why? What makes you so special?" I want you to put down all the reasons now and in the future why you are special.

MATTHEW: Okay, I'll give it a go.

MENTOR: I want you to remove the word *try* or similar words from your vocabulary. Start recognizing what words you're using. I want you to think of these types of words:

- Try
- Should
- Must
- But
- Maybe

These words are limiting you because they're allowing you to give yourself an excuse.

Where you say, "I'll try" isn't a commitment. To quote Yoda, "No. Try not. Do or do not. There is no try." It is either you're going to do, or you're not going to do. If you say you're going to do it, then do it. It's about taking that first step and getting in the right mindset.

You are starting to have realizations about yourself. I'm not going to tell you you're going to do one thing or the other thing. Then you're always relying on me. What I'm trying to build into you is an ability to be aware of your decisions and what is driving them.

MATTHEW: I also wrote down a few more things about things I think and say to myself. I did a little bit of that, though I felt a little bit strange. But I did find some things.

MENTOR: Oh, yes, that's right. Nice change of topic. How did that go?

MATTHEW: You said write down things I say or do when I'm in certain situations. Some of the stuff that I wrote down, I didn't really like about myself. I was saying things like when I was buying stuff, I was down on myself and I'd think, "You don't deserve that," or I'd say, "Oh, why are you buying that now?" Things like that.

This one time stuck with me, and it got me upset for quite a few days. It was a meeting when we were just discussing ideas at work, and I had an idea, and I thought it probably is a silly one. I didn't say it and I remember thinking—*This isn't a good idea. It probably won't work.* Things like that. I was sitting there for a while, and then five minutes later, one of my colleagues said the same idea. The nearly exact same idea. The manager thought that was brilliant, and that we should go ahead and do it. And then he asked that person to flesh out the idea and get it going.

I'm there thinking, *But I had that idea.* And I couldn't understand why I didn't say anything. Well, I could. I was thinking that it was a stupid idea and I didn't trust myself to say anything. That really made me feel, well, made me feel angry, and it made me feel sad in a way as well. Everybody thought it was brilliant, and that person got a lot of praise. And the worst thing was I had to say well done as well. I was feeling a little bit envious, but it was my own fault. My own doing.

MENTOR: Of the things we listed above, where does this fit?

MATTHEW: Fear of feeling foolish?

MENTOR: That's right. This is why I want you to write it down. I'm not trying to make you feel bad about yourself. It's great in one sense that you had that experience where it was a thought you had. You didn't say it, somebody else did, and then it was a positive experience for that person. And you felt dirty about yourself. Not great, but hopefully you can see that maybe you do have good ideas.

This is awareness. Next time you might speak up. Or you might not. Thank you for sharing. I know sometimes saying these things and admitting how you felt can be difficult. It's all about awareness. If we can bring these thoughts out and we can see the patterns that we have, we can slowly change them.

Nobody wants to feel like they're making a fool of themselves. But you know what? Those people that throw themselves into the things that they fear are the ones that are moving ahead and are being successful because they're not limiting themselves.

Always ask yourself, "What's the worst that can happen?"

MATTHEW: I can think of plenty.

MENTOR: Yes, we humans are good at that. But how many of them are likely?

MATTHEW: Probably not too many.

Matthew shrugs.

MENTOR: I think you need to continue doing this. Awareness is the starting point for any personal development. I know that some of these things might be a little bit difficult. I want to talk about one more thing here. At the beginning, you said you weren't sure how this was going to help build wealth creation. You probably think the only thing that you're doing for wealth creation at this point in time is the budget stuff and even there, what are we doing? Saving $250 a month.

What are we trying to do here? We're trying to understand your thoughts and your habits, and we're trying to break those down and build new, sustainable habits that will get you to not only consistently build wealth but also to keep it.

It's no use if I say these things to you but you don't feel it. You'll think, "This doesn't apply to me, so I don't need to do this." I don't want you to get to a point of success and then self-sabotage yourself because you don't think you deserve this. A lot of people get to a point where they think, "I've gotten there," and then they start to spend it like anything because they don't think they should have it and spending it is one way to get rid of the money.

Or if we talk in terms of your why, then you might self-sabotage when you're in front of a crowd of kids. And then people won't book you. I want to get those things out of the way so that when you get closer and closer to success, you'll embrace it and enjoy it. You'll see that you are worthy of it. And that's where we're trying to get you to, step by step.

I remember we also said something about a personality test. Did you have a look at that?

MATTHEW: No, I didn't get to that one. I started reading the book extract but then didn't write it down. I'll do that this week.

Fourth Session

MENTOR: What we'll do first, before we get into anything new, is review the tasks from last time.

MATTHEW: Thanks. I did the personality test. That was really interesting. I learned something about myself there. Based on the color system, I've got a lot of Blue in me, and some Green and some Yellow.

Blue is obvious, as I am a data analyst, so it goes with the territory, but there are other parts to me as well. I realized I am a bit of a showboat. It's just something that's part of me—I like to have a lot of control. I want to be part of the scene, but I also want to control the scene and direct everything. I didn't really know that about myself. Some of the results really resonated, and some things didn't. It's interesting that it doesn't come out at work, but at home and with friends, it's there.

MENTOR: Yes, it can be like that. Some things will jump out at you and you'll think, "Yep, this is who I am," and you wonder how they know you so well. And then other things are a little bit more like, "Yeah, maybe I do that a little bit." But what's important about it is the awareness. I don't need you to go through it all unless you want to, but it's really for your own understanding. You're the type of person who likes to be in the center of attention—at least in some circumstances. Sometimes with that comes wanting to have the best things because you want to show off a bit.

I didn't realize that I actually like helping people. That is the Green in me. I like or feel better when I've helped someone.

MENTOR: That makes sense. Based on things we have spoken about and how you act.

MATTHEW: I also did some reading. I read *The One Thing* you told me about it earlier.

MENTOR: Oh, yes. Part of my reading list. It's good that you are investing time in yourself. This is what happens. You start to know yourself and then you want to know more and then more. What did you learn?

MATTHEW: That was really good, and now I get it a little bit more. I've got a question now around my wealth goals and my wealth why. I understand now why we're doing that as well. And I've got that focusing question he talks about—"What's the one thing I can do such that by doing it, everything else will be easier or unnecessary?" That was really quite good. I actually used it the other day, and it helped me make a decision more quickly and easily. It was something as simple as going out to lunch with people. I thought about it and realized, no, this is actually not going to get me closer to my wealth goal. I went for the social element, but I brought my own lunch. I did that, and nothing really happened. It wasn't awkward or anything. I was just eating my lunch while they had theirs. We still had a good time and everything.

MENTOR: Matthew, that is fantastic. You're really starting to understand this and move forward. Like I said, a lot of times, it's just little steps, but it's great that you've used that focusing question and started to put it into practice. That's really good. Did you see the power of it? That's the real thing I want to showcase to you—that when you use something like that, it's not about taking away or denying yourself. It's about understanding what your priority is and having a guide.

MATTHEW: Yeah, I actually found it really easy. Normally I'd just forget about the lunch I'd made at home and brought in and go buy another lunch with the team. It was different this time. I said, "You have your lunch; just eat it." I put the money I didn't spend into my savings. I was doubly proud of myself. That was really exciting.

MENTOR: You're really killing it!

Your Turn

Working on yourself is a deeply personal endeavour and one that can be very daunting. Looking at ourselves in the mirror can be the hardest thing we ever do. However, it can also be the most rewarding. The most important thing to remember is to be kind to yourself.

There are a few places to start. Below are some questions that will guide on your initial path to self-discovery:

1. Learn more about yourself by taking a personality test. This can give comfort, but the explanations of your personality can also give insights on how to build on your strengths and overcome some of your weaknesses. This is a good place to start and will help you to explore further reading or exercises to help you.
2. Rank your values with sticky notes—leave them up and revisit.
3. Write down your thoughts on money. Try to answer the following questions:
    1. What do you think of money?
    2. If you were given $1,000, what would you do with it?
    3. Would you like a lot of money? What would your friends think of you if you did want a lot of money?
    4. What are some of the common phrases you think about money?
    5. What do you think of rich people? What do you define as a rich person?
    6. What do you think of the share market?
    7. What do you think of your landlord (if you rent) or the bank (if you have a mortgage)?

You don't become someone new overnight. You build who you are with daily choices, repeated in tiny ways. The personality insights, the sticky notes, the spending spreadsheet, the rules, the people you keep close—they all add up. Do that work, and your Reason will stop being an idea and start being the life you live.

You have now started your journey of self-discovery, probably the hardest journey you will make in your lifetime. Although it is important in your journey to wealth, it will be valuable in your day-to-day life as well as you learn more about yourself. This is also a lifelong journey. You never stop learning about yourself. Which brings us neatly to the last part of ROGUE—Endurance. Wealth creation is a marathon, not a sprint.

Notes

Notes

Notes

CHAPTER 5
E IS FOR ENDURANCE

Compound interest is the eighth wonder of the world. He who understands it, earns it; he who doesn't, pays it.

—Albert Einstein

Success is not final, failure is not fatal: It is the courage to continue that counts.

—Winston Churchill

So here we are—the last part of ROGUE: Endurance.

We touched earlier on the idea of compounding—that powerful force that turns cents into fortunes and small, steady actions into remarkable outcomes. There's truth in the saying that compound interest is one of the strongest forces in the universe. But it's worth remembering that it works both ways. It can build you up or quietly eat away at what you've built, depending on which side of the equation you sit.

In this chapter, we will take another look at compounding but also talk about the long term and how having that outlook can help you reach your wealth goals. Endurance is about having that long term mindset and allowing things to mature. A tree does not grow in a year; it takes years, decades even, to reach a strong tree that can withstand storms. That is the same for your wealth.

My Story

When I first set my goal of being financially free at fifty, I already had patience baked into it. I'd given myself twenty-five years. That's a long runway, and I knew it wasn't going to be a quick win. I also knew I had a lot of learning to do before I'd have much to earn. I wasn't a gambler, so there was no "lottery ticket" shortcut for me. What I did have was time—and the willingness to use it.

Once I started building some wealth, I bought my first property. My parents lent me a bit to help get started, and I paid them back quickly. Then I bought another one not long after. Those two properties became my "set and forget" foundations—I didn't tinker much; I just let time and rent do their thing.

Next came shares. I started small, buying in little parcels, and made sure the companies I owned had dividend reinvestment plans. It sounds like jargon, but really it just meant that when dividends came in, I bought more shares instead of receiving cash. Over time, that snowballed.

Meanwhile, I kept learning. I did courses on property and investing, read about offshore opportunities, and even looked into collectibles. I surrounded myself with people who knew more than me and could advise me well. One of the best decisions I made early on was taking a tax course. It saved me money for decades. I understood what could be claimed and what couldn't, and how to structure things legally and efficiently. It meant every financial move I made worked a little harder for me.

Endurance came down to two main things: discipline and delayed gratification. I kept my budget tight but realistic, always linking my actions back to that long-term goal. It didn't mean I stopped living—I traveled the world, visiting forty countries and living overseas for seven years. But every experience fit within a plan that still pointed toward financial freedom.

I never bought a new car—not once. It just didn't make sense. The moment you drive it off the lot, you lose 10 percent of its value, and you're stuck paying off a depreciating asset. I preferred to buy secondhand and pay cash. That one simple habit freed up huge amounts of cash flow over time.

Each step was guided by patience, learning, and a clear sense of purpose. Paying off my first property felt incredible. I could see that every brick in that result had been laid over years of consistent effort.

People sometimes talk about "getting lucky." I've never believed much in luck—at least not the random kind. My kind of luck was "forced luck." I was ready. When an opportunity came along—a property listing, a new IPO or a new share, a new collectible—I could act because I'd done the work beforehand. That's not luck. That's the result of endurance, the real magic behind wealth.

Staying the Course

Anything worthwhile takes time. The first time you try something, it's probably not going to be great. You'll make mistakes—plenty of them. The second time, you'll make fewer, or maybe new ones, because you've uncovered something you didn't even know you didn't know. Do that enough times, and eventually, things start to feel smoother. What once took effort becomes second nature. That's endurance—showing up again and again until the work becomes part of who you are.

It's also important to celebrate along the way. When you hit a small or big milestone—such as a property purchase, a solid return on shares, or even just sticking to your budget for six months—take a moment to recognize it. Not with something that derails your progress, but with something that reinforces it. When I hit a financial goal, I'd buy a book or take the family out for dinner—something that acknowledged the win without undoing the work. Celebrating wisely is part of staying patient.

Endurance is about the long game. It's about holding steady when progress slows, when the excitement fades, and when the novelty wears off. It's about showing up when it's boring and doing the work anyway.

This is the quiet magic of endurance. It's not dramatic or glamorous. It doesn't make headlines. But it's what separates the dreamers from the doers.

When I set my goal of being financially free by fifty, I knew it wasn't something I could rush. I built in patience from the start. Twenty-five years felt like a long time, but it gave me space—space to learn, to make mistakes, to let things grow. That's the key with any goal worth chasing: Give it time. Don't expect every year to be a straight lineup.

Markets dip. Plans change. Life interrupts. But if you keep your focus on the long term, those pebbles become just small ripples in a much bigger journey.

How do you stay the course? It sounds easy to say but for a lot of us, not easy to do. Here are some ideas:

- Keep a track of your financial habits to make sure you do them each day and see your progress—the Red X.

- Celebrate milestone achievements—if you keep going for a month or two months, then give yourself a little reward.
- Keep in mind why you are doing this (your Reason)—fantasize about what you will do with your wealth in the future
- Have someone you keep informed of your progress—a close friend, mentor.
- Give yourself a break if you mess up (now and again)—you can't let this become a habit, but if you misstep now and again, reframe as a learning exercise and get back to what you need to do.

I'll cover some of these in more depth below.

No Shortcuts

There are no shortcuts. That's something experience will teach you if you don't learn it early.

People love to say "talent" or "luck" explains success, but both only get you so far. The rest is just hard work.

Over the years, I've been tempted by the "Get there quicker" offers. You'll see them everywhere—investment schemes promising 30 percent returns in six months or systems that claim to beat the market. At first, those offers are exciting. You think, "If I can make three times my usual return, I'll hit my goal in half the time."

But it rarely works that way. I learned that the hard way. A few years back, when crypto was new, I got caught in one of those traps. I found a site that seemed legitimate—it had endorsements from celebrities and people I respected (though not for their financial skills). It all looked good. I tested it with a small amount—money

I was prepared to lose. The results seemed fine at first. I cross-checked the data, printed the reports, and compared them to real market movements. Everything appeared to line up.

Then came the invitation to invest more. No pressure, just a gentle suggestion. And it was working, so I did. For a while, the numbers looked incredible. Too incredible.

Even with all my financial education and discipline, I still wanted it to be true. That's the dangerous part—wanting it to be real. It wasn't. It was a scam. I lost six figures.

That loss taught me one of the most expensive and valuable lessons of all: Shortcuts don't work. They set you back. They prey on your hope and impatience. Real wealth—the kind that lasts—is built slowly, through education, discipline, and smart research.

Even when something looks perfect, step away, take your time, and think. If it sounds too good to be true, it probably is.

Endurance as a Mindset

Endurance isn't just about waiting; it's about how you wait. It's an attitude—calm, deliberate, focused. It's the quiet confidence that, even when the results aren't visible yet, your work is moving you closer to where you want to be.

That's why the R in ROGUE—Reason—matters so much here. When your "why" is strong, your Endurance is stronger. Organization gives you the systems to keep going. Gratitude reminds you to appreciate what you already have while building toward more. U (You) is the personal work that keeps you grounded.

Endurance is where it all comes together. It's the thread that ties the whole ROGUE mindset into something real and lasting. To create something of value normally needs time and effort, mostly the more time and effort, the better the creation. And the more fulfilling the creation will be.

Look around the world at examples, the best ones are old buildings—cathedrals or important structures, such as the pyramids, Christ the Redeemer, the Eiffel Tower, the Great Wall—they are truly amazing creations and they took decades to build and have stood the test of time. The same can be said for great works of art, scripture, and books.

The individual whose vision it was laboured long and hard to have their dream realized. Sometimes they were ridiculed for their vision or efforts; however, they kept going in the face of difficulties and made objects of world renown.

This is what you are doing here. You are creating something lasting, not fleeting. You are potentially creating a legacy beyond yourself, for children and grandchildren, and such things require time and persistence.

Distractions and Destructors

When you're building endurance, two of your biggest challenges will be distractions and destructors. Distractions are the everyday interruptions that chip away at your focus. Destructors are more dangerous—they're the people and influences that pull you off course entirely.

Some of these "influencers" may not mean harm, but they're not aligned with your goals. Their job is to sell, persuade, or entertain—not to protect your priorities. You're most vulnerable when you're just starting out. Once you've built momentum, it's easier to say no. But in the beginning, every temptation feels louder.

Distractions we have covered a little in organization when we talked about time management. We need to guard our thoughts and time closely so we can focus on the things that will get us closer to our Reason.

These are some distractors and destructors I have faced in my own journey:

- Friends and family trying to pull you away from your goals by making little comments such as:
    - *You're no fun anymore.*
    - *Why are you always working on that?*
    - *Is that more important than me?*
- Social media or the internet—we can get lost in rabbit holes easily. I know I have on many occasions—it is so easy. However, they are just a time drain and take you away from important activities
- Small items of little importance—this is a difficult one, as we all like little presents. However, how often do they just end up in the cupboard after one use? The money spent could have got you closer to your goal instead.
- TV/streaming—hours can go by watching TV or movies, and suddenly you are behind in what you wanted to do or what was important
- Household chores—this one is difficult, as things do need to get done for the household to function. However, make sure you don't get distracted by it to the exclusion of important things. The sense of achievement of household chores, since you can see your progress, can be seductive.

All of these have taken me away from things that were important for me to focus on for my wealth journey. However, we need to give things their time or to use them as rewards so they do not have power over us, but we have power over them.

The same principle applies to any goal: Remove friction, create structure, and distractions lose their power.

Falling Off the Wagon

Even with structure, we all stumble. You'll overspend or blow the budget on takeaway. It happens. What matters is how fast you reset.

Falling off the wagon isn't failure—it's feedback. Ask yourself what caused it: fatigue, stress, lack of sleep, boredom, frustration? Understand the trigger and adapt your system so it's less likely next time. The point of having Endurance is to realize that small missteps should not impact the long game or the long term horizon.

You will also not get everything right, and sometimes you just need to release some of that pent-up frustration, anger, or even energy. However, you need to do it in a controlled way and make sure you stay true to your long term vision. It is yours, after all.

When you fall off the wagon, reset. Understand it for what it is and make sure you continue on your journey. You are not going to have perfectly linear (straight) experience; there will be dips, jumps, and skips, but you will get there in the end as long as you restart back on your tasks after each stumble.

Celebrating Milestones

Patience doesn't mean waiting joylessly. Celebrating milestones—especially early ones—is an important part of the process. When your goal is a million dollars, your first $10,000, $25,000, or $50,000 are big achievements. Reward yourself—but do it wisely.

Celebrating the milestones provides you with a lift. It also indicates that you are proud of your own achievement. This is important and links back to Gratitude; however, whereas Gratitude is about keeping your mindset positive, a reward is more tangible.

Go see a movie with the family, get a message or facial, play a round of golf at a different course, take the family out for dinner, or mark the win in a way that supports your larger goal. The rewards can be spaced out over time—closer together at the start to buy good vibes and excitement, then wider as momentum builds and you don't need as much encouragement. That rhythm keeps motivation alive without sabotaging your progress.

Perspective

Endurance also requires keeping perspective. Life will have interruptions—health scares, family needs, or unexpected crises. Pause if you must, but don't quit. Remember that temporary detours don't erase long-term direction.

Keep your goal visible and keep asking: "Does this move me closer to it?" If not, you can confidently walk away.

This also helps when FOMO—the fear of missing out—creeps in. You'll see others buying new cars, taking big holidays, or upgrading their homes. You'll feel that twinge of envy. But stop and ask: "Do I really want that, or do I just want to look like I'm winning?"

True wealth isn't about signalling success—it's about substance. And Gratitude, once again, is the cure for FOMO. Be thankful for what's working, for what's growing, and you'll find that "missing out" doesn't sting as much.

The Red X

I've heard various versions of where this idea of the Red X came from. One version I heard was from comedian Jerry Seinfeld. When he was asked how he keeps coming up with jokes and updating his stage performances, he said he would write a joke every day—and maybe more. Every day he would put an *X* on the calendar to say he had done that job for that day.

He said he used a red pen. Initially, you might have two or three *X*'s, and that didn't make much of an impact. But you start doing a week or two weeks and you start having this chain of Red X's. And then in your mind, you don't want to break that chain. So every day you're doing everything to make sure you don't break that chain.

So how can this be used for your journey in wealth creation? This can be used in multiple ways, but what you're trying to build up is this consistency of the Red X. I suggest that you do something visual—whether it's a paper version of a calendar and you literally put an *X* in there.

Now, what the *X* represents is really up to you, but here are a couple of things related to wealth creation that you can use the power of the Red X to help you out:

1. Don't buy a cup of coffee. Every time you don't buy a cup of coffee, you put a Red X on that particular calendar day. Those Red X's mark up. You probably also need to make sure you're either saving that money or it's going somewhere else purposeful.
2. Small daily savings. You might have a small savings goal of saving a dollar or two dollars a day when you first start. You might have a bottle, and you might have a calendar

above it. Every time you drop in $2, you put a Red X there. "I did my savings goal today."

3. Track your spending. If you're writing out your spending habits, receipts, and expenses, you've got your little notebook. Every day you write down the things that you spent, you get a little Red X. You might have the calendar up there, the little notebook on the side, and every night you transcribe your receipts to that notebook and mark it off on the calendar.

You will find that you do not want to break that pattern. You do not want to break that trail of Red X's. While you're building up, you're creating consistency and habits. If you keep this going, you will get to the place that you want. This is one way that you can start this long game by introducing the Red X and continuing it.

As you transition and some of these things become automatic—"OK, I've done the coffee thing," or "I've done the savings, and that's working"—you might transition the Red X into something else and use it to move something else forward. You're still using that Red X as a guide.

For three months, you might do the coffee thing. Once you've done the coffee thing, you might use the Red X for savings. Once you've done savings, you might use the Red X for something else. Here are some next-level examples:

1. Reading a financial book. Read for thirty minutes a day. This can be important as you start to delve further into understanding yourself and wealth creation. You might read certain books to help you understand shares, property, whatever it is. You say, "I need to do thirty minutes or fifteen minutes," and every day as soon as you do that

reading, you put a Red X on the calendar. You can have the calendar up and the book underneath it with a red pen so that you pick it up, do your reading, and mark it off.

2. Research and investigation. If you want to do trading—shares, whatever—you might first need to do an investigation. You say, "Every day, I want to do thirty minutes of share investigation." You do that and use the Red X to make sure you're going to the share market, seeing what's happened for the day. Every day you pick out a share and you do some investigation of it, make some notes about it. Is it a good share? What's been said about it? As and when you have some money, you've already built up an idea of some shares that are worth investing in.
3. Weekly or monthly reviews. The Red X doesn't need to be a daily thing. It can be weekly or monthly. As you go through this process, you might want to review your spending habits or expenditure weekly or monthly. You might have it down for every Sunday. Every time you go through that and you've had a look at your expenses, you know what your expenses are, you know where your money is, you've matched it all up—you can then do a red X for that particular day and mark it as completed for that week or month.

Using the Red X in any of these ways, especially in wealth creation, is incredibly powerful because you do not want to break that chain. You want to keep it going. You really feel bad when you break the chain. I've been in this situation when I've had this, and I really felt bad about breaking it. You want to bring it back. The first time you do it, there's some guilt and some shame associated with that—not great emotions—but it impacts you. You want to use those in reverse to give yourself the pleasure of saying, "Look, I did it again."

These things build up, and this can be part of your gratitude. You can say, "I've done seven Red X's this week. I've done what I said I would do each day this week." That gives you that sense of satisfaction, and you can make it self-perpetuating by putting the Gratitude in there.

You might use the Red X for different things. It doesn't always have to be the same unless there's something you want to keep doing. You might use it first for not buying coffees or lunches, mark that down, and then move on to using the Red X for reading time, for learning, for education. Then you might move it onto asset exploring—looking at shares, researching investments. You might use the Red X in different ways as you move along this wealth-creation journey. That will help you keep that consistency. You can look back over the months and say, "Look, I am building this consistency of time and effort." That's really the beauty of being in the long game.

Looking at Compounding Again

It does not matter how slowly you go, so long as you do not stop.

—Confucius

One of the things about endurance and the idea of ROGUE is about letting time have its ability to affect your finances. I want to come back to this compound interest example. I've given some examples about how compounding is better than simple interest. Now I'm going to take two things we've talked about—the coffee example that we keep coming back to, and compound interest—and put those two together to give you an understanding of how compounding can really work.

In this example, I'll show you how compounding works over time. What we have is a coffee cost—let's just call it coffee, but it could be any item. I was a soft drink consumer and would very often buy a bottle of soft drink every day. Other people, it's coffee. For some people, it's a bar of chocolate. We all have little things we buy every day to give us a boost or a sense of fun, whatever it is. I'm going to use that as the thing we're going to remove.

When we remove it, instead of it just going back into our general money, we're actually going to save that. In this example, I'm going to say that's worth $5 each time we purchase it. We do that four days a week. The fifth day—Friday, or maybe Monday or Wednesday—we grant ourselves one day a week where we do buy it.

Table 5: Compounding Example 1: $5 Item, 4 Days a Week

Item Cost	$5
S&P500 Ave Return	8%
Interest Rate	3%

	S&P Return	Interest	Money Spent
Year 1	$1,046	$1,006	$984
Year 5	$6,186	$5,342	$4,920
Year 10	$15,444	$11,534	$9,840
Year 20	$50,041	$27,035	$19,680
Year 25	$81,084	$36,683	$24,600
Year 30	$127,548	$47,868	$29,520
Year 40	$301,180	$75,864	$39,360

For $5, four times a week—that's $20 a week we're saving. That ends up being about $80 a month, and about $480 every six months, roughly $960 per year. I looked up the S&P 500 average return over the last twenty years—it's about 8.4 percent. Other share markets are around that. The ASX is about 7.6 percent, and some of the European ones are around that as well. If we look at interest rates as a comparison, they're probably around 3 percent. That's what I'm using as a starting point.

Let's say you're early in your career, maybe in your twenties, and you're going to let this go for forty years. What is the difference if we did this?

In the first couple of years, probably to year 10, there's not a lot of difference. With the S&P, you've got about $15,000. With interest, you've got about $11,000. The money spent is about $9,000. You might think, "Well, I've only gained $6,000 in ten years. It's okay, it's something, but it's not amazing."

But this is where compounding starts to really ramp up. Even at year 20, just ten years later, you're now at $50,000 for the S&P return. Interest is now $27,000. And if you'd been spending—assuming everything stays the same price, which it normally doesn't—it's about $20,000. Now you've got a $30,000 gap between the S&P and the money you would have spent if you'd just spent it on this item continuously for those twenty years.

The one we really need to look at is year 40. Across those forty years, if we've done this for forty years—$5 for four days every week for forty years—we would have spent about $40,000. If we had just put that into a savings account, we would have made close to double that—about $76,000. Okay, that's not bad.

But if we put it in the S&P where there is real compounding going on—the interest is compounding, too, but it's at a very low rate—with the S&P compounding, we're up to $300,000. That's ten times the money we would have actually spent. That's an amazing amount of growth.

Table 6: Compounding Example 2: $10 Item, 4 Days a Week

Item Cost	$10
S&P500 Ave Return	12%
Interest Rate	4%

	S&P Return	Interest	Money Spent
Year 1	$2.145	$2,027	$1,968
Year 5	$13,628	$10,979	$9.840
Year 10	$37,644	$24,337	$19,680
Year 20	$154,561	$60,361	$39,360
Year 25	$286,017	$84,418	$49,200
Year 30	$517,688	$113,686	$59,040
Year 40	$1,645,503	$192,621	$78,720

Let's take this a little further. In this case, we've got $10. Maybe you're buying lunches, or maybe it's a coffee and a pastry in the morning, or something like that. It's a little bit more. Again, the same principles—you're buying it about four days a week across the time.

We've also now found something a little bit better than the S&P—the average return is 12 percent. We've also upped the interest rate to 4 percent to give you a better idea of what this could be.

Again, similar to the last time, not a lot different in year 10. We're all at about $20,000. We see a similar change to what we saw in the first example, but it's a little bit more. The investment at 12 percent is $37,000. The money spent is about $19,000. It's nearly already double.

In this case though, when you look at year 40, you would have spent $78,000 on coffee and a pastry, or lunches, or whatever it is. However, if you'd put that money into an investment and got that return of 12 percent, you would now have $1,650,000.

Wow. That is a big number. And all the money that you actually spent was just $78,000. So $78,000 turned into $1.6 million. That is really the power of compounding.

That's why it matters even if you start when you're thirty. Even if you've only got thirty years, you'd still have half a million dollars, and you would have only spent $60,000. That is an amazing level of return.

That's why compounding is such an amazing thing. It makes your money work. It makes it work for you and you don't have to do too much. You don't even have to look at it. You just have to keep putting that $10, that $20 per week or $40 per week into whatever it is. Keep building that up and it will slowly grow and grow and grow until it's got to a point where you don't have to worry about money ever again.

Now I would like to share with you a counterexample. In this example, we will have $100 per month that we invest and we look at two scenarios, one where we take our yearly savings on some item and add it to our savings and another example where we don't and see what the difference will be.

Table 7: Compounding Example 3: All Your Savings Versus Some Savings

Monthly Savings	$100
Item Cost per Year	$2,000
S&P500 Ave Rate	8%

	Return on Just Savings	Return on Savings plus Item Savings
Year 1	$1,276	$3,402
Year 5	$7,543	$20,116
Year 10	$18,834	$50,223
Year 20	$61,026	$162,736
Year 25	$98,883	$263,689
Year 30	$155,546	$414,789
Year 40	$367,292	$979,446

We have seen the difference time makes, but now we can see the difference that an extra amount of money makes per year. In the table above for the second column we are adding just an additional $2,000 per year (that's $80,000 over the course of the forty years), but the difference in the end result is astonishing. In both columns we have $48,000 we are saving over the forty years, and it is already amazing the amount that turns into.

However, adding the extra $2,000 puts us streets ahead in forty years time. In the first column, we end up with $367,292 whereas in the second column we are just short of $1 million. That is quite a difference. In both cases, it is only a small amount of money to reach those numbers—$48,000 or $128,000.

This is not rocket science—this is called patience.

That is what we talk about when we talk about endurance. It's keeping it in there for the long haul, allowing compounding to take effect. Interested in further perspective on compounding, read the excellent book *The Compound Effect,*[24] it has some more examples of compounding and the power it has to achieve great things.

A Client's Share Journey

I'm reminded of a client I had who, for different reasons, was not able to work anymore and couldn't get a decent pension from the government for disability due to their circumstances. They had to find something else to be able to generate money.

This was somebody who was good with their hands—a tradesperson. Good at figuring things out, good at working with their hands, decent intelligence, and also quite good at practical thinking. But a lot of their work in the past was hands-on. They weren't somebody who would do a lot with computers and things like that.

That world was basically cut off from them. Because of the incident that happened, there was no way they could go back to the work they were doing. After the usual time spent understanding what was going on and coming to terms with things, they went and started to study shares. They thought, "Okay, shares are something I can do at home. I can do it in a way that I want, and I have some control"—which was really something they wanted to have.

We worked with them to figure out how to do this and tried to instill in them that this was going to be a long-term venture. Just because you start trading doesn't mean overnight everything's

24 *The Compound Effect*—Darren Hardy

going to go well. There were going to be hiccups along the way. They really had to have, especially in the beginning, a mindset that this was going to take some time.

That was difficult because they had bills to meet on a day-to-day level, but they also needed to consider their future. They had some savings, some money put away, and that needed to work for both of those things while the share portfolio they were looking to build would eventually allow them to have some sort of income.

That mindset shift was the difficult thing to work through because there was that immediate need and also this idea that shares shouldn't be that difficult—"You just buy and sell. You can see what's going on." But they really had no thought process of what made a good share or not. They were later in their career, so this also meant they had to suddenly say, "Okay, I'm back at the level where I know nothing."

You've got somebody in a difficult situation where money is tight—not completely dire, but if nothing good happened, it could become a panic station. And in one sense, they were in a job where they were the top person, and now they're going to something where they're the bottom person. This is late in life as well. So there were two mindset shifts we had to work on.

We had to work with them to say, "Well, if you want to build this wealth, you have to embrace this student culture. Be the student again and don't think that you have all the answers. Otherwise, as they say in the share world or trading world, you're going to blow up your account, and you'll have nothing. You've also got to think about this in the long term and you've got to be dedicated to this."

We mapped out a plan where, during the day, they would spend some time doing shares—learning, understanding what the share market was, what it is about, and what makes a good share. They had some common sense and started off with logical things—blue chip shares that were designed to be something likely to stay strong. We were talking about the big banks and the resource sector, which are huge in Australia. They worked through those and got a base-level portfolio that would provide, over time, a level of income.

From there, they looked at other ways of working in the share market to understand another way of generating income. They had dividends and growth, but what else could they do? Over time, this person started to identify dividend scalping as one way they were quite willing and prepared to pursue. They also looked at start-ups—not IPOs, but once a share had been on the market for a while, maybe six months after all the IPO hype had run its course. If it was still a good share with good prospects and all the indicators looked positive, that would be something to buy for big growth in a short space of time while it was building up.

This was not going to be simple. Even though they had concerns about their income in the short term, this took them probably about two to three years to get going. They spent a good five hours a day learning about the share market in whatever format—reading, the internet, seminars, whatever it was. They went along because they knew this was what they needed to do. This was what they needed in order to create wealth.

Fast-forward probably twenty-five years later, and they had a portfolio close to $2 million. But if they hadn't spent that time at the beginning learning and understanding that this was for the long term—not just trying to get money in the short term—they probably would have blown up their account then and there.

The moral of this is: Understand where you're going and understand what your timeframes are so that you can make sure that you invest the time up front to make the end goal happen. If you don't do that, you're going to struggle to get where you want to go.

This is a little bit of an example of the stepping stones that you need to take. You might have the money and you might have a little bit of the nous, but you still need to continue your education. That's why endurance is so important—because your education continues to develop and you continue to learn. You're getting better and better at choosing investments, choosing loans, choosing whatever it is you're looking at because you understand more and more.

The first ones you do, you look back on later after maybe four or five years and think, *I could have done this a lot better*' That's what you've got to do. You've got to start small and build up and build up and build up. That's where endurance really pays dividends. If you don't take some of the work you're doing as a learning activity, you'll never learn, and you won't make better deals in the future.

Matthew's Journey

First Session

MENTOR: Endurance is a difficult one. However I want to ask you a question that might help illustrate it. Has anybody ever shared the compounding penny example?

MATTHEW: Penny example? No, I don't think I know that. What's the penny example?

MENTOR: I say to you, "I'll give you three million today. You can have it. Or if you wait thirty-one days, I'll give you this penny, and it will automatically double every day, and you'll get whatever it is at the end of that time." Which would you like? The three million or the penny that doubles?

MATTHEW: This is a trick question, isn't it? I think I would probably take the three million. But I know I probably should take the penny. I don't know how the penny's going to get to three million, though. I'm going to take the three million. Yeah, I know I'm going to regret this.

His mentor smiles and pulls out a small chart.

Table 8: Penny Example

No. of Days	$3,000,000	Penny Doubled (each day)
1	$3,000,000	$0.01
2	$3,000,000	$0.02
3	$3,000,000	$0.04
4	$3,000,000	$0.08
5	$3,000,000	$0.16
6	$3,000,000	$0.32

7	$3,000,000	$0.64
8	$3,000,000	$1.28
9	$3,000,000	$2.56
10	$3,000,000	$5.12
11	$3,000,000	$10.24
12	$3,000,000	$20.48
13	$3,000,000	$40.96
14	$3,000,000	$81.92
15	$3,000,000	$163.84
16	$3,000,000	$327.68
17	$3,000,000	$655.36
18	$3,000,000	$1,130.72
19	$3,000,000	$2,621,44
20	$3,000,000	$5,242,88
21	$3,000,000	$10,485.76
22	$3,000,000	$20,971.52
23	$3,000,000	$41,943.04
24	$3,000,000	$83,886.08
25	$3,000,000	$167,772.16
26	$3,000,000	$335,544.32
27	$3,000,000	$671,088.64
28	$3,000,000	$1,342,177.28
29	$3,000,000	$2,684,354.56
30	$3,000,000	$5,368,709.12
31	$3,000,000	$10,737,418.24

MENTOR: You are wise beyond your years to sense that. Yes, that's right. Look at the spreadsheet. As you can see, it starts as no contest. The $3 million all the way. However, toward the last couple of days, something magical happens. Compounding starts to work its magic. At the end of the thirty days, you are well in front, and after thirty-one, it is no contest the other way.

MATTHEW: That's amazing. I would never have thought that the penny would have gotten that high that quickly.

MENTOR: Yeah, it is amazing. Compound interest is the power you want working for you. Even with a smaller interest rate, it is still pretty good. This is what we are going to tap into. Have a look at this simple example.

Table 9: Difference Between Compound and Basic Interest Over the Course of a Year on 10 Percent Return

No. of Months	Compound Interest	Basic Interest	Difference
1	$1,000	$1,000	$0
2	$1,100	$1,100	$0
3	$1,210	$1,200	$10
4	$1,331	$1,300	$31
5	$1,464	$1,400	$64
6	$1,611	$1,500	$111
7	$1,772	$1,600	$172
8	$1,949	$1,700	$249
9	$2,144	$1,800	$344
10	$2,358	$1,900	$458
11	$2,594	$2,000	$594
12	$2,853	$2,100	$753

MATTHEW: Yeah—a bit of a difference. I can see that.

MENTOR: That's only twelve months. Continue those numbers, and the differences get bigger and bigger. The main ingredient is time. Time is what makes the magic.

MATTHEW: There's no quick win here in terms of what I should do.

MENTOR: No, there's no quick win. Quick wins are also quick loses as well. I want you to sit with this for a while. You're an analyst. Do some more number crunching. See where you get to.

Second Session

At the end of their second session, they talk more about Endurance.

MENTOR: How did you go with the compounding example?

MATTHEW: I did some more investigation. With even a small rate of return, you can make some big money from a small amount.

MENTOR: Yes, that's what I want you to realize. Time is your best friend. Once you have a saving plan and you stick to it, you then need to create an investment plan.

MATTHEW: Investment plan?

MENTOR: I'm not a financial planner, so I can't give you financial advice. You might want to talk to one eventually. However, an investment plan is a personalized, written strategy that maps out your financial goals, risk tolerance, and time horizon to guide your investment decisions. It outlines how you will allocate assets (stocks, bonds, cash, property) to build wealth, manage taxes, and ensure financial security while helping you stay disciplined.

MATTHEW: Is that another textbook talking?

MENTOR: Yes, again, they are good to get the right definition. But let's break that down into the key components:

1. Goals
2. Assets to invest in

3. Taxes
4. Time horizon

We are working through a lot of this. Endurance as part of ROGUE is the time horizon. Know that as you have a long time horizon, you will get to your goal. However, if you want a shorter time horizon, then you might have to put in more money. See this example here.

Table 10: Time Versus Money Trade-Off (Assuming Interest Rate of 5%)

	Amount (in $) per month			
Time (in Years)	$20	$50	$100	$200
5	$1,366	$3,414	$6,829	$13,658
10	$3,119	$7,796	$15,593	$31,186
20	$8,255	$20,637	$41,275	$82,549
25	$11,960	$29,900	$59,799	$119,598
40	$30,648	$76,619	$153,238	$306,476

MATTHEW: I can see that.

MENTOR: You can always get there quicker, but you need to make your money work harder. Your assets, whatever they are, need to give you a better rate of return. This is the work you need to do. You need to research over time:

1. How do you minimize taxes?
2. What asset classes to invest in? Property? Shares? Bonds?
3. How much risk can I stand?
4. How much money am I going to invest in these assets?

I can only guide you here. This is where some of the work needs to happen. However, you know that you will reduce your debt in fourteen or so months, so you have that time to start to get yourself knowledgeable.

You can see there are layers upon layers upon layers of this as you grow and as you get into it. First, you need to have that plan about saving. Then you need to make sure that money is working for you. At the moment, it's okay in the bank, but once it hits four figures—which, based on what you're doing, will happen very quickly—you need to get more information. And you need to get good information. You need to make sure that you're going to reputable people and that you understand what you're doing.

MATTHEW: I need to do the research myself.

MENTOR: This is wealth creation. It's not about handing it off to somebody else. It's about you taking ownership of it. Once you know enough, then you can hand it off to somebody else because you'll know whether what they're telling you is the truth. Right now, if you hand it off to somebody else, you don't know whether they're doing a good job or not. If they come back and say, "Oh look, I got 2 percent growth for you," you might think, *Well, that sounds bad.* But if you don't know the market, that might actually be quite good at that point in time.

Third Session

MENTOR: Hi, Matthew. How did it go?

MATTHEW: Yeah, I had a little bit more time this month. It's been a little easier for me to do some of the things. I read some books and better understand what I need to do. It just seems to take so long.

MENTOR: Yeah, I understand that. But think about it like this, okay? Think of Michelangelo when he was painting the Sistine Chapel. It wasn't there straightaway. He had to think about it. He had to imagine it. He had to put in a plan, and then he had to go through each of those steps in that plan to get that goal completed. It took him seven to eight years.

Wealth creation is not something that happens overnight, and it's also not something that happens by itself. You have to have a strong foundation to ultimately get where you want to go. What we've been doing so far is building that foundation so it'll last long term. If I just came in and told you exactly what to do, you would have no ownership of it, and you would take no responsibility for it. We're trying to actually build up where you take ownership and you understand why you're making changes. So even when you hit inevitable barriers, you'll be able to keep going.

Wealth creation is step by step. But it is also about keeping the long game in mind. There are a few things you can do to help you here. I want you to try one of them.

MATTHEW: Okay.

MENTOR: Every time you save $1,000, I want you to give yourself a little reward. Nothing big. And nothing that costs a lot of money. It might be good to come with a few rewards that you can use at different times.

MATTHEW: I can do that.

Fourth Session

MENTOR: How did you go with those rewards? To help you keep on track?

MATTHEW: Yeah I came up with a list. Here it is:

- Go to the movies.
- Go for a walk in the forest with my dog.
- Take my partner to lunch.
- Take my partner for a coffee (and maybe a cake).
- Buy a book on investments.
- Listen to a podcast from an investment guru.
- Go to a spa.
- Workshop or class on a special interest topic.
- Board game.
- App game or in-app purchase for something.
- Karting.
- Tennis or squash game.

MENTOR: That's a great list. I'm sure you can add some more as time goes on. I want you to allocate one reward to each significant saving milestone. That way, as you start to see savings grow, you will reward yourself for your persistence. You will also see what your next reward will be and start to try harder.

As you get bigger savings, you might want to switch this to investment rewards. As you make your money grow via investments, you could give yourself a reward. For example, when you earn your first $100 from an investment, you get a reward or you make your first investment and so on.

MATTHEW: I'll think about that.

Your Turn

This might be a little more difficult to see practical steps for Endurance; however, there are a few things that you can do to make this something to see.

Here are a few things that you can try to help build endurance in your life:

- Do the Red X for weekly (or monthly) saving goals.
- Write out a list of rewards for milestones along your journey; they can be different types or values for different types of milestones.
- Do some analysis on how your savings might grow based on different interest rates / timings /amounts to see how it might differ (I provide an example spreadsheet if you provide me with your email address; details at the end of the book).
- Make a list of distractions that might cause you to go off course.
    - Create a list of things you might do to avoid or reduce their impact.
- Create an entry in your calendar to review your Reason on a monthly basis.

This might not seem a lot but it will help to keep you on track and to be aware of things that might stop you from seeing the benefits of compounding.

Notes

Notes

Notes

THE FINISH LINE (AND BEYOND)

If there's one truth I've learned, it's that there's never really a finish line. When you reach one goal, another takes its place. And that's a good thing—it means you're still growing.

Endurance is about living in that space—continuing the journey, learning from the process, and knowing that every day you show up, you're compounding not just your wealth, but also the journey of self-discovery that you are embarking on. The lessons that you learn along the way will provide you with the knowledge for growth and understanding that will shape you in the years to come.

Each lesson or mistake that you learn from will make you a more resourceful, open, and curious person, which will help grow your wealth. They will stimulate each other.

There's no overnight success, no sudden arrival. There's just the quiet satisfaction of seeing the plan unfold, one step at a time, until one day you look back and realize how far you've come.

That's the power of endurance. That's the ROGUE way.

Conclusion

The real measure of your wealth is how much
you'd be worth if you lost all your money.

—Anonymous

Now that we've gone through ROGUE, the next part of the journey is really up to you.

Wealth creation is not something that happens in a moment. As you work through the topics in this book, you will not only grow your wealth, but you will also grow as a person. You will know yourself much better. You will be able to understand how you operate, what works for you, and what doesn't work.

The wealth that you create through reaching your goal, through your growth, and through the gratitude that you embrace in your life—that is the true wealth that you create.

Be kind and be true to yourself, and you will succeed.

Your journey starts now.

The ROGUE Way

We come full circle:

R—Reason: Know your why.

O—Organization: Build systems to make progress inevitable.

G—Gratitude: Stay grounded and thankful along the way.

U—You: Do the inner work; growth starts from within.

E—Endurance: Be patient, persistent, and ready for the long game.

Each piece strengthens the others. Together, they form the mindset that turns ideas into independence. Wealth, after all, isn't just about money—it's about freedom, discipline, and living life deliberately.

That's the **ROGUE** way.

BOOK CITATIONS (AND DETAILS)

Byrne, R. (2006). *The secret.* Atria Books/Beyond Words.

Carroll, L. (1865). *Alice's adventures in wonderland.* Macmillan and Co.

Clason, G. S. (1926). *The richest man in Babylon.* [Originally published as pamphlets starting in 1926; compiled into book form in 1926]

Clear, J. (2018). *Atomic habits: An easy & proven way to build good habits & break bad ones.* Avery (Penguin Random House).

Duhigg, C. (2012). *The power of habit: Why we do what we do in life and business.* Random House.

Erikson, T. (2014/2019). *Surrounded by idiots: The four types of human behavior and how to effectively communicate with each in business (and in life).* St. Martin's Essentials. [Originally published in Swedish in 2014; English translation 2019]

Hardy, D. (2010). *The compound effect.* Vanguard Press.

Hill, N. (1937). *Think and grow rich.* The Ralston Society.

Keller, G., & Papasan, J. (2013). *The ONE thing: The surprisingly simple truth behind extraordinary results.* Bard Press.

Kiyosaki, R. T., & Lechter, S. L. (1997). *Rich dad, poor dad: What the rich teach their kids about money that the poor and middle class* *do not!* TechPress, Inc. [self-published]; later published by Plata Publishing.

Nafousi, R. (2022). *Manifest: 7 steps to living your best life.* Michael Joseph (Penguin).

Newport, C. (2016). *Deep work: Rules for focused success in a distracted world.* Grand Central Publishing.

Robbins, A. (1986). *Unlimited Power: The New Science of Personal Achievement.* New York: Free Press.

Schwartz, D. J. (1959). *The Magic of Thinking Big.* Prentice-Hall.

URGENT PLEA!

Thank You For Reading My Book!

I really appreciate all of your feedback and
I love hearing what you have to say.

I need your input to make the next version of this
book (and my future books) better.

Please take two minutes now to leave a helpful review on
Amazon letting me know what you thought of the book.

Thanks so much!

- Stefan Kuegler

www.ingramcontent.com/pod-product-compliance
Lightning Source LLC
LaVergne TN
LVHW050930210926
848482LV00013B/594
* 9 7 9 8 9 0 0 5 7 4 0 0 4 *